Praise for Kayleen Reusser's books:

We Fought to Win: American World War II Veterans Share Their Stories (Book 1, World War II Legacies)

"This book documents the experiences and sacrifices of Hoosier veterans who are a part of The Greatest Generation." Christopher Wiljer, librarian

**

They Did It for Honor: Stories of American WWII Veterans (Book 2, World War II Legacies)

"The information shared from the hearts of 34 World War Two Veterans, is simply stunning. Being a 'veteran' myself (Vietnam), and a long-time appreciator of the 'service to mankind' concept, this book really got my attention." Curtis Rose, sculptor

We Gave Our Best: American WWII Veterans Tell Their Stories (Book 3, World War II Legacies)

"The stories are written in short, easy-to-read biographies and are eye-witness accounts ranging from their wartime experiences to heartwarming memories. The stories are enhanced by photos and timely explanations of WWII history." Shana Neuenschwander, librarian

**

D-Day: Soldiers, Sailors and Airmen Tell about Normandy (Book 1, World War II Insider)

"The author has pulled from first-hand stories of those that were there … (to tell) what it was like to be among the first to wade upon the shores of Europe for the end of Nazi terrorism." Harold Wolf, Amazon Top 500 Reviewer

It Was Our War Too

Youth in the Shadows
of World War II

Witnesses of War Book 1

Kayleen Reusser

Kayleen Reusser

Kayleen Reusser Media

It was Our War Too: Youth in the Shadows of WWII.

First published in the United States by Kayleen Reusser Media.

Printed in the United States. Copyright © 2019 by Kayleen Reusser

KayleenReusser.com
ISBN 978-1-7325172-3-3

Cover illustration by Kayleen Reusser
Printed in the United States of America
The information provided within this book is for general informational purposes only. While the author has tried to provide correct information, there are no representations or warranties, express or implied, about the completeness, accuracy, reliability, suitability or availability with respect to the information, products, services, or related graphics contained in this book for any purpose. Any use of this information is at one's own risk.

Photographs are courtesy of National Archives, individuals as named and the author.

Acknowledgments

Writing a book about history can be a challenge. I appreciate when others step up to assist. Thanks to Wells County Public Library, Wabash County History Museum, Allen County Public Library, Marion Public Library, Monroe County History Center, Bletchley Park, Indiana University Libraries University Archives, and Huntington City Township Public Library for help with these stories.

Thanks to Allen Shaw for sharing his book that provided geography of the European landscape during the early part of the 20th century.

Thanks to the World War II veterans who shared photos of the war for this book: Charles Dunwoody, Gabe Delobbe, Dennis Butler, Keith McComb, Fred Odiet.

Thanks always to husband, John, who supports me with shopping, cleaning, cooking, chauffeuring, banking (he loves that part), loving veterans and stories about World War II as much as I do. I could not do it without you.

Introduction

What was it like as a 10-year-old having a cannon shell come through your home? How terrifying was it to run with your family from the enemy? What nightmares did you suffer from watching people freeze to death?

During World War II, millions of people from approximately 60 countries around the world faced the reality the war -- starvation, exposure to danger, homelessness, separation from families and other terrors. As difficult as it is to consider, many of these people were children.

In addition to the hardships of survival, some children lost family members, resulting in lifelong pain. Other youth contributed time and energy to supporting those doing the fighting.

World War II did not just produce hardship. For some it brought love.

No matter the situation, each young person discovered World War II directed their lives in ways he or she could not have imagined. They not only survived but thrived in individual circumstances.

The idea for this book developed over the past decade while I conducted interviews with hundreds of World War II veterans. They and others shared stories about people they knew who had been involved with the war as civilians --a Resistance fighter, child evacuated out of London during the Blitz, falling in love with an American soldier, and more.

Their stories, while not taking place on a battlefield, has relevance and a place in world history. It was satisfying to pull their tales together into this volume to present them as part of our national heritage.

A few of the people profiled here are people I've known for years (one was a childhood neighbor; another I took knitting lessons from). Most are new acquaintances, people I now hope to call friends.

These stories, like those of the veterans in my earlier books, are intended to lend a greater appreciation of the meanings of freedom, patriotism and courage.

If you know someone whose story would fit into a future volume of a Witnesses of War book, contact me at KayleenReusser@gmail.com.

Contents

Map of Europe ca. early 1940s

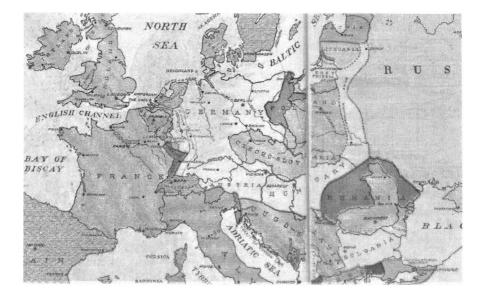

Note: After World War II, East Prussia was divided into Russia and Poland and ceased to exist.

Some spellings of countries are different than what is used today, such as Jugoslavia and Rumania.

The map is from <u>Freedom's Triumph: The Why, When</u> <u>and Where of the European Conflict</u> published by Woman's Weekly, Chicago, 1919.

Gabriel Delobbe
Belgian Resistance Fighter

On May 10, 1940, 14-year-old Gabriel 'Gabe' Delobbe's heart pounded as German tanks thundered through his hometown of Charleroi, Belgium. He knew from listening to neighbors that his country's small Army had no chance of overcoming the Nazis. The residents stood, silent and helpless, as the enemy quickly took control of their beloved country.

At first Germany's occupation was not hard on the Belgian people. For two months little changed -- then the German Army began confiscating food, shoes, and other supplies, whatever they wanted.

The Belgians were reduced to strict rations that included more than food. "The hardest item to lose was tires," said Gabe. "Without them we could

not go anywhere, but there was no gas so it didn't matter."
Belgians rode electric street cars, bikes or simply walked.

By 1942, the German military controlled Belgium's radios, newspapers, and factories. "It was illegal to listen to news from the British Broadcasting Corporation," said Gabe. "Some of us tried, but those caught were killed."

"In the factories they were building V1 and V2 rockets," said Gabe. "I didn't want to be part of that."

Everyone between the ages of 16 and 50 was required to work for the Germans. When given the choice between working in a German factory or a coal mine in Belgium, Gabe chose the coal mine. "In the factories they were building V1 and V2 rockets," he said. "I didn't want to be part of that."

During the war, many European cities experience fighting and destruction, ca. 1944. Photo by Gabe Delobbe.

In early June 1944 Gabe was in a mine when he heard that Allied forces had invaded the beaches of Normandy. Determined to help his country, he quit his job and joined the Underground, a resistance movement of French and Belgian citizens formed to fight the Nazis. "I signed up as a volunteer for the duration of the hostility," he said.

Allied vehicles and troops drive through France after securing the country's liberation in September 1944. Photo by Gabe Delobbe.

For two weeks Gabe and other young men from Belgium trained at a Catholic school in France. "We learned English phrases, how to carry and fire a M1 Garand rifle and use grenades," he said.

That summer Delobbe lived in the Ardennes Forest of Belgium with others in the Underground. The group sabotaged trains loaded with German troops and supplies. "We used dynamite, but it was bad to work with," he said.

Instead, the rebels unscrewed train rails, splitting them so trains went off the tracks.

Gabe and other members of the Underground were helped in their efforts by Belgian farmers. "We only trusted people we knew," he said. "If a person asked too many questions, we thought he or she could be a German spy." Gabe eventually worked for the American First Army as part of the Allies, helping to liberate France in September 1944. He wore an American helmet and arm bands that identified him as an Ally. "I wanted to be recognized as a friend to those fighting for France," he said.

> *As the Battle of the Bulge progressed and supplies dwindled, Gabe and other soldiers wore shoes made from cardboard.*

For his efforts as a saboteur Gabe was paid $1.50 per day by the American military. "We in the resistance received 'issue' money," he said. "We couldn't carry real money in case it fell into German hands."

In December 1944 Delobbe participated in the Battle of the Bulge in the Ardennes Forest. The surprise attack by the Germans caught the American Army woefully off-guard. "Most GI's had thought the war was almost over," he said.

Allied troops were ill-equipped for the extreme cold-weather with temperatures below zero. "The snow was up to our knees," said Gabe. As the battle progressed and supplies dwindled, he and other soldiers were forced to wear shoes made from cardboard.

In January 1945 Gabe assisted in the escape of an American major and two sergeants. Another time he helped shoot down a German single-engine fighter plane using small-arms fire.

In April 1945 Gabe was involved with the Battle at Remagen Bridge and liberation of the German concentration camp of Buchenwald.

Allied troops move through a French city after heavy damage by Allied artillery and air support. Photo by Gabe Delobbe.

When German forces finally surrendered in May 1945, Delobbe was at Remda, Germany. For several months he guarded German prisoners of war awaiting trial.

"I was told by an Army officer that if anyone tried to go in or out, I should shoot to kill," he said. When a group of German officers were led away as prisoners, he guessed they were headed to a trial in Nuremberg.

In December 1945, after a year and a half of fighting on behalf of the Allies, Gabe Delobbe was discharged from the American Third Army. He had received minor wounds on three occasions but was otherwise unharmed.

In January 1946, the Belgian government re-organized its army and Gabe enlisted. He took the place of American guards at a prison full of German soldiers. "When we arrived as replacements, the GIs were allowed to go home," he said. Sergeant Delobbe was discharged in May 1946.

In 1952 Delobbe and his wife Colette sailed to North America, settling in Fort Wayne, Indiana, where Gabe made a career as an engraver and photographer, skills he had learned from his father.

In 1957 the Delobbes became American citizens. They are parents to two daughters (one is deceased).

For his help in World War II Gabriel Delobbc was awarded a Distinguished Service Cross and silver and bronze medals. He is a member of the Society of the Remagen Bridge and the American Legion.

"I was thankful to have contributed to the effort of the Allies in the war," said Gabe. "At 20 years old I never thought about being scared. My family has loved living in America and we hope we have made it a better place for everyone."

Eileen McShane Garey
Operation Pied Piper

Adolf Hitler's conquest of Poland in September 1939 and England's subsequent declaration of war on Germany and the Axis Powers created fear in the British people. Would Germany attack in an attempt to force them to surrender?

With the possibility of an invasion looming, England created a plan to protect their children, especially those who lived along the country's coasts. Organizers encouraged residents of less risky areas further inland to allow children from the cities to live with them. The volunteers would be paid to shelter the children. The plan was called Operation Pied Piper.

With only a small bag of clothes, snacks, drink, and gas mask (issued to people of all ages, including babies) children – often entire school classes -- were transported to their destinations, usually by train.

Eileen McShane was four years old when she was registered for Operation Pied Piper. She and her parents lived in Liverpool, a large port city in the northwest part of England. Liverpool had warehouses and a railway system that connected to industrial cities like Birmingham, Coventry, London and Southampton.

Eileen Garey and her brother William pose for a photo, ca. 1945.

A shipyard was a short ferry ride on the opposite side of the River Mersey in a town called Birkenhead.

Eileen and her mother, Margaret McShane, rode in a car from their home to an unknown destination in the country.

Members of a London Auxiliary Fire Fighting Services perform a war exercise in London, ca. July 1939.

William McShane, Eileen's father, stayed behind. The family's plan was that William would continue working at his butcher shop in Liverpool. At night he volunteered as an auxiliary firefighter combating fires caused by the bombs.

When the McShanes said good-bye, they did not know when they would be together again. After several hours. Eileen and her mother arrived in a village where a local farmer and his wife provided a run-down cottage for them to live in.

While the cottage had been declared condemned, due to the country's extreme shortage of housing it was considered fit for evacuee accommodations (Eileen cannot recall the names of the couple or the village).

Eileen and her mother were required to register their ration books for food with the local butcher. Ration books contained coupons for portions of bacon, ham, butter, cheese, margarine, cooking fat, milk, sugar, jam, tea, eggs, candy.

Lines to receive rations for food, like meat and sugar, become a common occurrence in England, the United States, and other countries.

"We were allowed one egg, four ounces of beef, and two ounces of tea per week," said Eileen. Meat would continue to be rationed through 1953.

As vegetables were not rationed, home owners were encouraged to grow carrots, cabbage, cauliflower, beans and Brussels sprouts in gardens. Across the British Isles large swaths of public parks were divided into allotments and leased to the public for vegetable gardens.

While it was comforting to be away from the bombs and mayhem in the city, Eileen and her mother quickly became homesick. "The couple we stayed with showed us kindness," she said, "but the farm was quite isolated. There was no warm running water and only an outhouse."

"We children who had been forced to leave our homes didn't feel sorry for ourselves," said Eileen. "We just knew that was the way it was."

In the fall of 1939 Eileen and her mother returned to Liverpool. However, in May 1940, another attempt by the Luftwaffe (German Air Force) to obliterate Liverpool caused mother and daughter to again flee to the country. This time they were offered two rooms with a family in North Wales. "We were given a bedroom and parlor and shared a bathroom with the family," she said. "We ate in our parlor after the family was done in the kitchen."

Eileen attended school in the village. "Teachers added classes to accommodate all of the evacuees," she said.

Although homesick, Eileen refused to cry. "We children who had been forced to leave our homes didn't feel sorry for ourselves. We just knew that was the way it was."

Eileen recalled her father's words when he joined the British Royal Navy: "I am not going to let others fight my war for me."

In September and October 1940, Hitler ordered the Luftwaffe to drop hundreds of high explosives and incendiary bombs nightly on British homes, docks and railways. Thousands of people died and hundreds of buildings were demolished in cities and villages.

St. Paul's Cathedral in London escapes destruction in December 1940 during a nightly fire raid.

Despite the devastating onslaught and devastation, the British people did not surrender. The bombings, and valiant British defense, especially by air, that eventually fought off the attack became known as The Battle of Britain.

In June 1941, Hitler turned his attention to an invasion of the Soviet Union. Margaret, who had known she was pregnant before the move, returned to Liverpool with Eileen. She gave birth two months later to a son, William. Their family was again separated when Eileen's father joined the British Royal Navy. "He said he was not going to let others fight his war for him," said Eileen. William McShane was posted to various duties before being assigned as a gunner on a naval destroyer.

As his son's condition worsened, William's father was granted compassionate leave. "We feared my brother would die," said Eileen.

William's absence meant extra responsibilities for Margaret. She not only had to care for Eileen and Baby William but she manage the butcher shop as well. "One of my aunts worked in the shop with Mom, while the other cared for me and my brother, as well as her three sons," said Eileen.

Challenges for the McShane family increased in spring 1945 when a dysentery epidemic ran rampant throughout England's cities, leaving the country's undernourished children especially susceptible. Eileen and three-year-old William were admitted to a hospital.

As William's condition worsened, his doctor petitioned the Royal Navy to grant his father compassionate leave. "The doctor feared my brother would die," said Eileen.

On May 8, 1945, nine-year-old Eileen and other children in the hospital were led to the auditorium. "The doctors and nurses were laughing and the place was covered with Union Jack buntings," she said. "I wondered what was going on."

The hospital staff had big news. The war was over! On that date, which became known as VE ("Victory in Europe") Day, Germany signed its surrender to the Allies.

An excited American soldier hugs an English woman while surrounded by happy faces of service men and civilians at the war's end, May 1945.

A feeling of great relief and excitement filled the hall. "I knew Dad would come home soon," said Eileen. Shortly after VE day, Eileen and her brother were discharged.

After receiving news about his son's health, William McShane sailed to Sydney, Australia, before obtaining a place on a military transport for England. The five-day journey ended with a train ride from London to Liverpool.

Though weak from their illnesses, the McShane children's spirits lifted with their father's return. William McShane resumed his work in the family's butcher shop, which remained open for many years.

In 1956, Eileen McShane married an American soldier and moved to the United States. Today, she lives near New Orleans where she volunteers at the National World War II Museum. Each year she gives talks to schoolchildren about her role in Operation Pied Piper.

"I tell them that if the Americans had not come into the war, England could not have held up," she said. "I volunteer at the museum because I recognize and honor the bravery of the people who served in my native country and in the United States. If not for them, we would not be here today."

Hilda Welker Gutwein
Hitler Youth

By the time Hilda Welker was five years old, she felt as though she lived in a war zone. Born in 1932, she and her family lived in Yugoslavia in an area known today as Serbia.

The soil her family farmed was rich and the area earned the nickname 'Wheat Chamber of Europe.' Hilda's ancestors had relocated there from Stuttgart Germany in the 1770s.

That same land caused trouble. Hungary desired it and the residents alternated being ruled under both countries' flags. When Hilda, her parents and seven siblings (she was the youngest as twin sister Luisa was born first) moved to the town of Cervenka, Hungary, the government gave them a plow, horse and land. In exchange Hilda's family gave the government ten percent of their income from the farm. "As a child, I learned to speak Hungarian, Yugoslavian, and German," said Hilda.

Refugees carry loads of personal belongings while fleeing on foot from Hitler's oppressive government. Photo by Keith McComb.

Land was not the only thing people fought for.

In 1933, after Adolf Hitler became chancellor of Germany, radios, phones and newspapers were prohibited. Most of the news the residents received was propaganda designed to accomplish Hitler's agenda, which was controlling people's minds. When he invaded Poland in September 1939, Hungary sided with Germany as an Axis Power.

Hilda's family, who attended an Apostolic Christian Church, tried to resist Hitler's laws. In the late 1930s the German government required those not Jewish to boycott businesses owned by Jews. Hilda's family and her parents didn't believe in Hitler but felt helpless. "People who tried to exercise freedom of press or speech usually disappeared," she said.

> *When the German military rounded up Jewish people to take them to prisons, Hilda's family realized how much control Hitler had gained.*

At the start of World War II, all German males between the ages of 16 and 60 were drafted into military service. Hilda's three older brothers were sent to fight. Conrad was stationed in Austria. Ed was captured and sent to a Russian prison. Ludwig died in Finland. As Hilda's father, Ludwig Welker, had served the German government for seven years in World War I, he did not have to fight.

When the military began rounding up Jewish people to take them to prisons and work camps -- some of them neighbors and friends of the Welkers -- Hilda's family realized how much control Hitler had gained. "My parents decided we must leave Hungary," she said.

It would not be easy. By 1944, many people were leaving their homes with wagons and on foot, filling the roadways on their way to Switzerland and other neutral countries for sanctuary.

As Luisa suffered from severe asthma, her parents arranged for her and Hilda to ride a train with Hitler Youth who were being evacuated to safety. Luisa and Hilda, now 12 years old, had been members of the government-mandated organization since age six.

This woman cannot conceal her misery as she dutifully salutes Hitler's forces now in control of her city.

Hitler believed youth were the future of Germany. He required children to attend Hitler Youth meetings which included girls and boys playing games and learning outdoor skills. "We were taught about Adolf Hitler, such as where he was born and his birthday," said Hilda. "Mom and Dad didn't like him but I kept my opinions quiet."

As Luisa and Hilda packed suitcases (one held food; the other clothing), they trembled with fear and sadness. "When we didn't know if we would ever see our family again," said Hilda.

> **At Hitler Youth meetings girls and boys learned about Adolf Hitler, including where he was born and his birthday.**

Her parents hugged their daughters good-bye at the train station. "We will be together soon," their father told them. "Remember what you have been taught and look to Jesus. No one can take what is in your heart and mind."

The children rode the train to refugee camps outside of Vienna, Austria.

The camps were full so a kindly married couple offered their home to the twins. For the next few weeks, Hilda and Luisa attended school at the camp.

As the war drew closer, the youth were moved again, this time to Czechoslovakia. Through a series of events, the Welker sisters were joyously reunited with their family in the city of Gerlitz.

Devastation of European cities makes housing scarce. Photo by Charles Dunwoody.

The Russian military was still headed west. When Ludwig desperately tried to purchase train tickets for his family to Dresden, Germany, where refugee camps were established, he was turned away. The train for Dresden was full. "We'll pray and ask God for guidance," he told his family.

> *When Ludwig Welker tried to purchase train tickets for his family to Dresden, he was turned away. "We'll ask God for guidance," he said.*

A few days later, the Welkers boarded another train to Dresden. In the city a horrific scene greeted them. An

Allied air raid had dropped phosphorus bombs, resulting in the deaths of approximately 500,000 people -- one-third of the city's inhabitants.

"If we had ridden that first train, we would have been caught in that catastrophe," said Hilda. "Our family prayed for the families of those killed." In May 1945, the war in Europe was over but the Welker's fight to survive continued. In Austria they shared a small house with three families, each given two rooms in which to eat and sleep. "We stood in line each day at 3:00 a.m. for food," said Hilda.

> ### *During harvest, Hilda worked 10 hours a day for farmers in exchange for a dozen eggs or kilogram of butter.*

Each day after school, Hilda and Luisa gathered firewood for heating and cooking. "As refugees, we were not given permits to cut trees like the nationals, but we did have permission to gather limbs from the forest floor," she said. During harvest, 13-year-old Hilda worked 10 hours a day for farmers in exchange for a dozen eggs or a kilogram (approximately two pounds) of butter.

At age 15 Hilda found work as a dental apprentice. Her employer provided meals, which allowed more food for her family. "I walked four miles to work each day for three years, grateful for the job," she said.

After the war, seven members of the Welker family applied for visas to go to America. In 1951, after a six-year wait, their visas arrived when a church in Francesville, Indiana, offered to sponsor them in the United States.

The Welkers mowed yards, worked as housekeepers and did whatever jobs they could find. "I learned English by reading children's books," said Hilda. She eventually found work as a dental technician for an American dentist.

In 1959 Hilda married an engineering student named Erwin Gutwein. Three years later, they became parents to a daughter.

In 1961, Hilda and her family were sworn in as American citizens. "We promised never to be burdens to the United States government," she said.

Hilda and her daughter wrote a book called "Time to Choose, Growing Up Under Hitler and Watching History Repeat Itself."

"I still believe in our family's Christian teachings and pray our nation will draw near to God and ask for His forgiveness," said Hilda.

Anna Mae Quackenbush Hudson
Rosie the Riveter

During the summer of 1944, Anna Mae Quackenbush walked each morning from her home in Bedford, Indiana, to a nearby gas station. Upon arriving, the teen hitched rides with local truck drivers who took her to the RCA plant south of Bloomington.

Before the war, the 1.5-million-square-foot RCA factory had been built for construction of radios. In the 1940s, it was converted for the manufacture of war materials. "We all helped each other because it was for the war effort," said Anna Mae.

She was the second of three daughters born to Frank and Rose Anna Quackenbush of Bedford. Frank was a stonecutter but later would become a business owner. Anna Mae and her sisters, Rosemary and Phyllis, attended Girl Scout meetings led by Rose Anna.

As a teen, Anna Mae Hudson works at a factory making war materials. The job would earn her the title as a 'Rosie the Riveter.'

A student at Bedford High School, Anna Mae did well in classes, especially Latin. She planned to attend college to study geology. But there was a war to be fought first. Although the war with Germany was being fought round the world, Anna Mae and other youth of Bedford were aware of its import.

Over the years, they had showed support for the Allies by participating in scrap drives, saving paper, tin cans and even aluminum gum wrappers, all of which could be used for war materials. Frank Quackenbush and other adults served as Air Raid volunteers.

"We kids may have been young," said Anna Mae. "But we were close to the war."

As the war continued, its effects became painfully real. One day a visitor arrived at the door of Anna Mae's English class. "He told our teacher that her brother had been killed," she said. Another time the people of Bedford were saddened to learn a former resident, Johnny Blackford, 18, had been killed overseas. "We kids may have been young but we were close to the war too," said Anna Mae.

She became even closer to the war when in spring 1944, three men in suits had entered the school to speak to the female students. "They offered us full-time jobs on an assembly line for the summer," she said. Male students were not considered as potential employees as their services would be needed as soldiers.

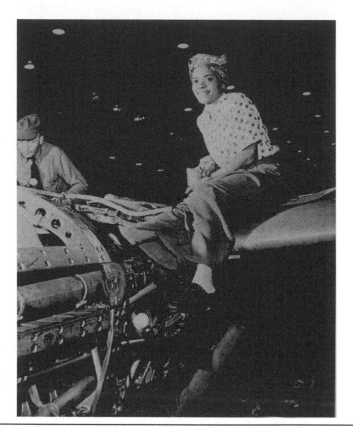

A riveter at Lockheed Aircraft Corporation in California prepares a plane to be flown by Allied forces.

When the men in suits stated the wages to be paid to workers, Anna Mae sat up. The RCA job would pay better and offer more hours than her previous summer jobs at a movie theater and city pool.

Although the men didn't specify what the assembly line work involved, Anna Mae didn't care. Nor did it bother her that none of her friends wanted to apply for the job. "I had just celebrated my sixteenth birthday and was anxious to try something new and meet new people," she said.

Anna Mae applied for the RCA job and was hired, along with hundreds of other females. Their routine rarely varied as they sat, day by day, facing each other in long lines, putting pieces together to assemble they knew not what.

> **By working at her job in the factory, Anna Mae accomplished two goals -- saving money for college and contributing to the war effort.**

When their day ended at 5:00 p.m., they clocked out and headed home. After eating dinner and socializing with her parents and sisters, Anna Mae went to bed, preparing to repeat the same actions the next day. If the 16-year-old quickly became tired of the repetitive actions of assembling parts, it didn't show. Anna Mae contented herself knowing she was accomplishing two goals -- saving money for college and contributing to the war effort.

One event broke the monotony.

Near the end of the summer Anna Mae and three other young women were taken off the line by a supervisor. Led to a room, the trio were each handed a paper and told to read the words typed on it. They appeared to Anna Mae to be directions for putting together parts for a machine. "We were asked to determine if anything in the instructions appeared to be incorrect," she said.

During the war, American women work at jobs making war materials. It is the first time their contributions play a part in a military conflict.

The workers did as they were told, studying the reports meticulously. Upon finding no errors, they handed back the papers with the solemn promise not to divulge their activities of the last hour, nor the contents of the forms.

Anna Mae returned to her position in the assembly line, avoiding the curious glances of co-workers and saying nothing about what had happened during the past hour. For years after the war, she told no one, not even her family, about the unusual request.

Why were Anna Mae and the others picked as proofreaders? "I can only imagine it was because I was a good reader and understood the information quickly," she said.

When the job in the RCA building ended at Labor Day, Anna Mae and the other teens returned to school. Not until years later would she learn about the mysterious piece she had helped to construct at the RCA building by the all-woman operation.

The piece which the women had nicknamed 'Madame X' was a top-secret, new device called a proximity or V-T fuse. The V-T fuse operated electronically on the end of a missile. The fuse sent out sensors. Rather than wait for the missile to make contact with an approaching target before exploding, the sensors sent a message to the fuse, causing the missile to explode mid-air with maximum impact.

Before the war's end, the Allies used V-T fuse missiles in the European and Pacific Theaters and in London to combat German bombings of the city.

A year later, Anna Mae transferred to Indiana University before returning to Bedford to work at Naval Support Activity Crane near Bedford as a secretary.

In 1947 she married Warren Hatfield who served as a Navy SeaBee in the war. They become parents to one daughter. Anna Mae stays busy with family and friends. Hobbies have included reading, membership in Bedford's

Women at Douglas Aircraft's Long Beach, California plant prepare airplane noses for A-20 attack bombers.

Rock Club and community groups. The work she and other female workers performed in munition and war supply factories across the United States earned them a special name and drawing that would become a cultural icon. They were referred to as Rosie the Riveters.

In April 2019, the Indiana General Assembly recognized Anna Mae and the other 10 million women who worked as Rosie the Riveters during the war, acknowledging their contributions.

Although Anna Mae's job at the RCA building occurred more than 75 years ago, it remains important to her. "Many of us may have just been kids at the time, but we were part of the war," she said. "It was all we thought about. It was a terrible thing and we all wanted to win."

Melba Thorn Jackson
Husband MIA

Eighteen-year-old Melba Thorn Jackson stared at the Mother's Day card in her hands. Her sister-in-law, Georgia DePoy, had received the note in the mail at her home in Huntington, Indiana. To anyone else, the card would not appear frightening. But something about it had so alarmed Georgia that she rushed to Melba's home.

Melba understood Georgia's concern.

The card contained no signature or message. On the envelope the sender had penned Georgia's address. But instead of her name, he or she had written her sister-in-law's, Melba.

Melba was the wife of Georgia's brother, Gerald. A student at Union Township High School in Huntington, Melba planned to graduate the following May.

Against her family's wishes, 17-year-old Melba Thorn elopes with Gerald Jackson after he receives his draft notice.

Against the wishes of her family, Melba had eloped with Gerald Jackson, a farmer four years her senior, in October 1942, shortly after he was drafted into the Army. Melba loved Gerald and believed as his wife, she would be kept informed of his whereabouts during the war.

Immediately after exchanging nuptials, Gerald had left for boot camp training at Camp Croft in South Carolina. Melba continued to live with her parents and attend school. She wrote to her new husband often, praying for his safety.

After completing boot camp with the United States Army, Private Gerald Jackson sails to the Pacific.

For several weeks, Melba and Gerald kept in touch via letters. This allowed Melba to know after completing boot camp that Gerald had traveled by troop train to San Francisco before boarding a troop ship to Australia with thousands of other replacement troops. Gerald had written as often as he could and Melba treasured each response.

Then, inexplicably, the letters stopped.

For five months Melba received no word from Gerald. Melba's father tried to lighten her mood by singing a mournful country tune entitled 'No Letter Today.'

In April 1943, Melba's worries increased when a stack of her letters sent to Gerald in Australia were returned, unopened. When she took her concerns to the Army, officials tried to reassure her. "They said he was probably on the move and unable to write," she said.

> **Melba refused to believe Gerald was dead. "I knew he would come home but not in a box," she said.**

Melba tried to stay positive. "I refused to believe Gerald was dead," she said. "I knew he would come home but not in a box."

The unsigned card Melba held in her hands which had been sent to Georgia offered the first clue to Gerald's whereabouts.

As Melba and Georgia examined the return address on the envelope, they noticed it had been sent from Darnall General Hospital in Danville, Kentucky. Neither Georgia nor Melba knew anyone who lived in that area or worked at the hospital.

Despite the card being unsigned, mailed by an unknown person from a hospital in a different state, the women felt hope.

The handwriting on the envelope was familiar. Both women had seen it in other correspondence, though not for several months.

It was Gerald's.

Hoping the card had not been sent as a misguided joke, Melba and Georgia contacted the local chapter of the Red Cross. Maybe someone there could help them discover who had sent the card. If it was Gerald, what was he doing at the hospital and why had he contacted them so mysteriously?

U.S. troops clamber from a combat transport to landing barges in preparation for an upcoming Pacific invasion, ca. November 1943.

A few weeks later, the sisters-in-law heard from the Red Cross. "They told us the card had been sent by a patient at the hospital," said Melba. The patient, who had been there since early March, was diagnosed with a severe mental illness. His identity was unknown.

Melba and Georgia were convinced the patient was Gerald. Hurriedly, they made plans to visit the hospital, purchasing bus tickets to Danville and arranging time off for Melba from her job at a munitions factory in Huntington. Georgia found friends to watch her children.

> *Gerald didn't recognize Melba or even his own name.*

The women rode the bus to Danville, checking into a hotel before hopping on a street car to Darnall Hospital. Throughout their journey they had prayed that the mystery would be revealed and Gerald – if the patient who had sent the card was him – would be in good health to return home.

When Melba showed hospital staff Gerald's military serial number, which she had written down to prove her identity and that of his, they agreed she and Georgia could meet the patient. Melba nearly collapsed upon viewing the man lying in bed.

It was Gerald!

Sadly, he didn't appear to recognize Melba or Georgia. He didn't know his name, nor did he recall sending the card.

When Melba showed him family members from photos she had brought, Gerald exhibited no response.

Privately, the medical staff told the women the few details they knew about what had happened to Gerald Jackson prior to his illness.

From Australia Gerald and other soldiers had sailed to the island of New Guinea. The invasion there against the Japanese had begun in January 1942 and would continue through August 1945. Gerald and other troops were sent in as replacements.

Palm trees lend a relaxing feel to islands in the Pacific, but nurses and medical staff work long hours to restore soldiers to physical and emotional health. Photo by Fred Odiet.

No one knows what happened the day Gerald Jackson took refuge in a foxhole during combat. At one point it is believed he discovered the soldier he shared the dugout area with was dead, killed by an enemy sniper.

When Gerald was found in the foxhole, he was delirious with a fever of 108 degrees. Military medical personnel diagnosed him with malaria.

The terror of the proximity of death, combined with a fever may have compelled Gerald to tear off his dog tags, worn around each soldier's neck as a means of identification, and fling them into the dense jungle.

Deep into his delirium, Gerald could not identify himself. A search by military officials for the dog tags turned up nothing. At that point the soldier known as Gerald Jackson ceased to exist. The Army had a seriously ill soldier to care for with no name.

Believing the soldier had suffered a nervous breakdown, medical officials packed his body with ice while strapping him in a straitjacket.

When the soldier was able to travel, the military returned him to the United States for intense medical care, first to a hospital in California, then Kentucky.

As the Army had no way of identifying the soldier, officials could not contact his next of kin to relay his developments.

The staff relayed one unusual fact about the patient they now knew as Gerald Jackson. Although he didn't speak much, he did talk about one person -- Adolf Hitler. This seemed odd as Gerald's theater of operation had been in the Pacific, not Europe.

This Marine shows signs of battle fatigue after serving in the Pacific, ca. February 1944.

Regardless of his mental state, Melba loved her husband and wanted him home. During the next few days, she and Georgia visited Gerald often. However, their presence seemed to agitate him so that the staff had to strap Gerald to his bed.

When Gerald developed a fever, possibly as a recurring bout of malaria, his doctor suggested the women return to Indiana and allow Gerald to heal on his own.

> *As the weeks passed with Gerald making little progress, Melba felt discouraged. Would she ever have her husband back?*

Devastated, Melba received assurances from the doctor that her husband would soon be well enough to travel. "They said he could be admitted to the Veteran's Administration (VA) Hospital in Marion, Indiana," she said. The hospital, about an hour's drive from Huntington, would be close enough for Melba to visit him often.

Gerald arrived at the hospital in Marion on May 25, his birthday. "He had no uniform or personal items," said Melba. "Everything that had belonged to him had been lost overseas."

With Gerald now close by, Melba visited him each Wednesday after work, riding a bus, then trolley to the hospital. As the weeks passed, Gerald seemed to make little progress. Melba felt discouraged. Would she ever have her husband back?

Gerald's physician raised her spirits. "He said Gerald was getting better," she said.

One day when Melba went to visit Gerald, she knew something had changed. "He remembered everything," she said. "I saw a different husband."

In November 1944 Gerald was released from the VA hospital, while at the same time being discharged from the Army.

Gerald and Melba moved into their own home. Melba continued working at the factory while Gerald recuperated and resumed farming. They became parents to a daughter. Over the years, Gerald suffered from malaria attacks. He died in 1989.

Melba credits her church, Zion United Brethren Church in Huntington, and the local community for providing support to her family during the challenges with Gerald's health. "I could not have gotten through it without them and my own faith that Gerald would come home alive," she said.

Note: During World War II, military hospitals admitted 1.2 million troops for psychological and neurological damage, nearly twice the number admitted to hospitals for battle wounds.

Joan Wojciechowski Johnson
Father Killed in Action

When 12-year-old Joan Wojciechowski arrived home from school in late October 1944, her heart nearly stopped before speeding up again so she could scarcely breathe. She recognized the tan-colored form in her mother's hand. Joan had heard about Western Union telegrams, hand-delivered to homes, often carrying distressing information during war times.

This one was no different. The telegram stated Joan's father was missing in action.

Joseph Wojciechowski was born in Fort Wayne, Indiana, in 1909. The son of Polish immigrants, he had attended St. Peters Catholic High School. Not long after meeting Gladys Williams, a native of Fort Wayne, the couple had married. They became parents to four children—Joan, Stephen, Stanley, and Max. Joseph had been employed as a steam shovel operator prior to being drafted.

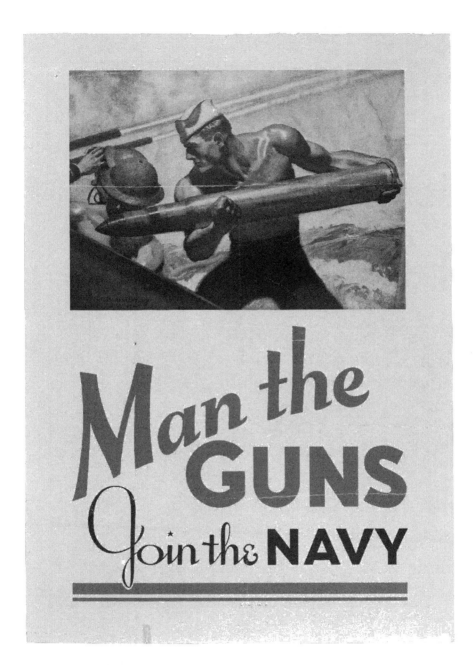

Man the GUNS Join the NAVY

The Wojciechowski family knew from his letters that Joseph, 35, had completed basic training at Great Lakes Naval Training Station near Chicago. Nearly twice the age of most other recruits, Joseph had been assigned to the USS *St. Lo*, an escort carrier with duties in the Pacific.

Possibly hoping to avoid the draft, Joseph had served in the Naval Reserves. But the U.S. had been at war with the Axis Powers since 1941. Three years later, all American men between the ages of 18 and 64 were required to register for the draft.

Soon after receiving his draft notice on May 3, 1944, Joseph Wojciechowski left Fort Wayne to join the United States Navy.

> ### *The crew of the St. Lo put up a valiant effort following a Japanese kamikaze attack, but the ship sank in 30 minutes.*

Joan, her mother Gladys and three brothers immediately began praying for his safe return. Now the form in her mother's hand threatened to disavow their prayers.

The telegram stated that in the early morning hours of October 24, 1944, the *St. Lo* became engaged in battle with Japanese forces near the Philippines during the Battle of Leyte. At approximately 1100 hours a Japanese kamikaze pilot attacked the *St. Lo*, striking it with explosive devices. Although the crew of the *St. Lo* put up a valiant effort, the ship sank in 30 minutes.

Crews of neighboring ships rescued hundreds of survivors from the water. Thirty later died of injuries. Of the 889 men aboard, approximately 113 were killed or missing in action.

Second Class Seaman Joseph Wojciechowski was one of those declared missing.

A search of several weeks turned up no sign of Joseph. A few weeks later, the American military declared him officially dead.

Despite crew members scanning the skies to locate enemy planes, kamikazes are difficult for Allied naval crews to detect.

Gladys Wojciechowski and her children held a memorial service for Joseph at their church. Her father's death caused Joan to struggle with her faith for a few years. "Though I was raised to believe in a loving God, it was a challenge to keep Him in my life," she said.

Joan was helped at coming to terms with the death of her father by recalling favorite memories. "Dad used to dress me up and take me on walks," she said. She knew her father had not wanted to leave his family and that he had missed them. In one of his letters Joseph wrote that he planned to get his children something special upon returning home. "He wanted to buy us bikes," said Joan.

The military awards $10,000 in life insurance to the family of Second Class Seaman Joseph Wojciechowski (sitting atop a piece of machinery) which they use to purchase a home.

As her husband's beneficiary, Gladys was given $10,000 in life insurance from the United States government.

Gladys later attended college to become a Licensed Practical Nurse, enabling her to earn a good income at a local hospital. It also offered her the opportunity to purchase a larger home to raise her family.

Gladys received marriage offers over the years, but she always refused. "My mother preferred her independence," said Joan, who helped with the family finances by working at a grocery warehouse and rubber factory while attending New Haven High School.

In 1949 Eagle Magazine, representing the fraternal organization of the same name, wrote a feature story about the Wojciechowski family and how they had coped after Joseph's death. Photos of each member of the family were printed.

A copy of the Eagle magazine, Joseph's two Purple Hearts (he had been injured prior to the attack) and a few photos are all that remain of Wojciechowski's life, although his legacy in the military continued through Steven and Stanley who both served during the Korean War.

In 1951, Joan was married and she and husband, Felix, became parents to three children. They cared for Gladys in the latter months of her life as she suffered from cancer, eventually dying in 1987 at age 74.

As the last living member of her family – all three of her brothers are deceased, Joan is alone in remembering the caring father who chose to honor his commitment to his country, resulting in a grieving family being left behind.

"I've thought about my family often over the years," she said. "They are not with me in body, but they're never out of my thoughts for what we went through together."

G TARZAN role is demonstrated by Max, youngest of the four children. | BIKE RIDING STEPHAN, the oldest boy, gives his vehicle a thorough checkup. | SAILOR SUIT STANLEY invites his brothers, sister: "Come and get it."

L' SWIMMING HOLE, an abandoned water-filled sandpit nearby, is a favorite rendezvous for the four Wojciechowski youngsters, all expert swimmers.

EAGLE FATHER Joseph Wojciechow went down with his ship in Pac

i would have wanted his family to n the struggle to carry on, the chowskis, like other war-bereft families, have discovered a staunch in the Eagles Memorial Founda- he future no longer looks as dark

kids love the outdoors, and in New Haven, right at their very doorstep, there is plenty of it.

Joan, 17, is the oldest. She's a blondish, buxom girl, strong and nice looking. When Joan had an operation for removal of

Stanley, 13, powerful and stocky, pl to be a farmer. And lean, tawny Max, the "baby" of the family, an expert sw mer, has visions of being a life gu What Max likes about school, as he p

In 1949, the Wojciechowski family is featured in an issue of Eagle Magazine, highlighting their resilience following Joseph's death during the war.

Alex Jokay
Resilient Refugee

Elizabeth Jokay was frantic. The Jokay family lived on a 3,500-acre country estate in the Hungarian village of Komárom, a city that lay on the south bank of the Danube River. The Jokay estate, including a horse farm, had been in the family for generations and forty families worked there.

But six years of war had changed their world. By January 1945, the German army was being beaten back and Allied aircraft bombed Hungary's industrial cities. The Russian Army was advancing and tales of Hungarian civilians being forced into cattle cars to be taken to Russia to work in slave camps ran rampant.

The thirst for revenge by the Russian Army began in 1939 when Soviet officials signed a non-aggression pact with Germany. Hitler refused to honor the agreement and over the next few years, sent soldiers to invade the country, killing millions. By 1945, the Soviets were moving west, seeking revenge on Germany's allies, including the people of Hungary.

As a child, Alex Jokay is surrounded by great wealth. Never could he or members of his family have imagined a few years later they would be homeless and starving due to the war.

Elizabeth Jokay feared not for her own life but that of her two sons, 17-year-old Louis and 14-year-old Alex. She and her husband, Miklos, had already lost one son to war.

Sixteen-year-old Miklos, named for his father, had volunteered to join the Hungarian army, thinking it was his duty. Sadly, the teen was captured and imprisoned in a French prisoner of war camp where he eventually died and was buried in a mass grave.

Elizabeth wanted her two remaining sons out of Hungary. Her two sisters agreed to accompany Alex and Louis across the border, along with a male cousin and young man who worked for the Jokay family.

Elizabeth stayed behind with her husband, Miklos. For many years Miklos Jokay had been a member of Hungary's politics in parliament. As conditions worsened in Europe, Miklos became severely depressed. "Father was afraid we would starve and become beggars," said Alex.

Miklos' condition became so severe that he was hospitalized. When Miklos left for the hospital, it was the last time his sons would see him. Louis managed the estate in his father's absence before leaving Hungary. Miklos Jokay died in 1945.

> *The war in Europe caused Miklos Jokay to become severely depressed, afraid his family would starve and become beggars.*

Alex, Louis, their aunts and the two young men took little with them when they left, joining thousands of other travelers streaming westward, away from the advancing Russian Army. As border controls no longer existed, the group easily crossed into Germany. There the group slept in a railroad cattle car.

Following Germany's surrender in May 1945, the Jokay family settled into a refugee camp in the village of Julbach.

Alex (left) and Louis (right) Jokay flee from Hungary with friends and family as the Russian Army invades. Their companion in the middle is unidentified.

Although the Jokays and friends were no longer in danger, survival was a constant challenge. After relocating to Munich, they lived in a former army barracks. "Nothing was left in the city but chimneys," said Alex.

For three years, the Jokays worked any job they could find. Food was especially scarce. "We had not starved in Hungary," said Alex. "In Germany we starved."

Yet returning to Hungary was not an option. In every letter Elizabeth implored her sons to stay away. What she didn't reveal was how much suffering she and others experienced. When the communist government moved in, they confiscated the Jokay properties. Elizabeth searched for a way to support herself.

Before the war, her husband had been a great supporter of the Hungarian Reformed Church. When church officials offered Elizabeth a job as a cook in a church-supported girls' school, she accepted, despite not knowing how to cook.

> *"My mother was a very strong-willed person," said Alex. "She survived in spite of hardships."*

As the Jokays had always employed cooks, Elizabeth had been relieved of those duties. Nevertheless, she worked hard. "My mother was a very strong-willed person," said Alex. "She managed to survive in spite of hardships."

Refugees use available resources like the river for washing clothes. Photo by Keith McComb.

In 1949 Alex wrote to his mother with exciting news. He had accepted a scholarship offer to attend Glenville State College in West Virginia. "I told her I was going to

America and not to worry," he said. He planned to major in English and history.

It was not difficult for Alex to make friends in his new American home, as he had been taught English in Hungary.

When friends encouraged Alex to apply to law school at Indiana University in Bloomington, he did so. There he met and fell in love with Sharon Davis from Fort Wayne. Following graduation, they married and moved to Fort Wayne where Alex was hired by Lincoln National Life Insurance Company in 1958.

> *Later in life, Alex's classmates from Hungary wanted to know why he had fled the country. "Their stories of survival convinced me it was good I had gone," he said.*

After becoming an American citizen in 1954, Alex was drafted into the U.S. Army where he served in the legal department.

In 1990 Alex retired from Lincoln after being promoted to vice-president and put in charge of the mortgage loan department.

Louis also moved to America after receiving a scholarship to Berea College in Kentucky. He developed a career as a food technologist.

Elizabeth feared she would never see her sons again. But in 1956 she moved to the United States to live with Alex and his family until her death in 1976. Her sisters, the aunts who had traveled with Alex and Louis from Hungary, also moved to the United States and worked in Detroit as domestics and in hospitals.

In 1990 Alex returned to Hungary and visited with former school friends. There, he discovered the true extent of what had happened to his native country. "My classmates wanted to know why I had left," he said. "Then I listened to their stories of survival and was glad I had gone." He learned the Russians had occupied Hungary until 1990. In the first years they took many people to Russian labor camps. "I am sure that had we gone back it would have happened to us."

Alex recalled one letter he received from his mother when he and Louis lived in Munich. She wrote that she believed she and Alex's father had failed their sons. Alex wrote back, refuting that claim. "I told her she could not be more wrong," he said.

"I believe one's attitude in life matters more than anything. My parents' attitude of success was what had mattered to me. I was 18 years old when I wrote that and I still believe it today. Sometimes life was a challenge, but I always felt like I could be successful."

Johannes and Marianne Klaffke
Running from the Enemy

In the dark hours of January 19, 1945, a rumble reached the village of Mehlsack in East Prussia. For nine-year-old Johannes Klaffke, his six siblings and mother Anna the sound could not be distinguished – Allies or Axis? No matter, the result would mean trouble.

During air raids over the past several months, the Klaffkes and their neighbors had watched in horror as homes, businesses and other buildings in Mehlsack were destroyed, including the school where the Klaffke children attended.

While Johannes had feared who would reach their village first -- Allies advancing from the west or Russians from the east – now it no longer mattered. The damage to be inflicted on them and the rest of the village would no doubt be severe.

The noise outside increased to a menacing growl as it neared the homes and businesses of Mehlsack.

As bombs demolish yet another building in Europe, the extent of war becomes overwhelming. Photo by Keith McComb.

Suddenly, an explosion ripped through the Klaffke's kitchen wall. Shards of glass from the window flew in dangerous fashion and the Klaffkes clutched each other, crying out as a Russian cannon ball landed in their midst.

The enemy had arrived.

When Adolf Hitler took over Germany in 1933, Johannes' parents had not agreed with his punishment of Jews and other groups, including special needs individuals and gypsies. But caring for their 11 children had taken precedence over worrying about politics.

When Johannes' father, Albert, died in 1937, friends and family members helped Anna and her children tend their farm, providing food and supplies. "Mother said she was glad Father was dead because he probably would have been thrown into prison for speaking out against Hitler," said Johannes.

> *At the Baltic Sea the Klaffkes crossed a frozen lagoon. When wagons broke through, people drowned.*

After the attack on their home, Anna and her seven youngest children hurriedly packed their bags. Four older Klaffke children lived away from home.

The Klaffkes would head west, joining an estimated five million displaced Germans seeking refuge wherever it could be found.

For the next couple of weeks, the Klaffkes trudged wearily through towns, sleeping wherever they could, eating little and relying on the kindnesses of strangers to survive.

At the Baltic Sea they crossed a frozen lagoon along with thousands of other refugees. In some places the ice became brittle, due to the weight of bodies. "Wagons broke through and I saw many people drown," said Johannes.

The Death March took its toll. "We were all so cold and hungry," said Johannes. "Mothers with babies had no breast milk to feed them. When the babies died, the

A group of refugees seeks safety from bombings and invasions with a handful of belongings. Photo by Dennis Butler.

mothers threw the little bodies on wagons to be buried in a mass grave." When Russian planes fired on the group from overhead, thousands of people fell, their dead bodies soon freezing.

In late January 1945, the Klaffkes tried to obtain tickets to head west on the Gustloff, a luxury ship belonging to Hitler. The ship, launched in 1938, had served as a hospital, then barracks for soldiers. To the thousands of exhausted refugees who clamored to board the vessel it shone like a beacon of hope.

The Klaffkes tried to purchase tickets on the Gustloff but were unable. Anna, a deeply religious woman, prayed for her family's safety. She and her children solemnly watched the Gustloff and its 9,000 passengers disembark, heading west.

> **The torpedo attack on the Gustloff became the worst maritime disaster in world history.**

The next morning the Klaffkes and others in the port received horrifying news -- nine hours after leaving port, the Gustloff had been torpedoed by Russian submarines.

Only 996 of the original passengers survived the explosion and the ship's sinking into the cold water. The attack on the Gustloff is considered the worst maritime disaster in world history.

When the crew of one of the last German war ships, the Admiral Scheer, offered the Klaffke family passage, it seemed Anna's prayers had been answered. "The crew gave us food, including bananas and oranges," said Johannes. "We hadn't seen those for years."

The war ship took them to the Oder River in Germany. But their situation again changed as the Russians broke through the German defensive lines and the captain of the Admiral Scheer was ordered to help. The Klaffkes moved to a smaller ship sailing south.

Out of money and nearly out of food, the Klaffkes struggled to stay optimistic.

A deeply religious woman, Anna Klaffke prays for her family's survival during their long sojourn across Europe.

"We were thrilled to find a single sausage at the bottom of one of our packs," said Johannes. "We shared it between us."

By the time the Klaffkes arrived in the town of Magdeburg, Germany, in March 1945, they were unkempt and infested with lice. They rode a train to Göttingen where one of Johannes' sisters, Helene, lived with her in-laws. City officials in Göttingen put the Klaffke family on a bus to the German village of Roringen. There in April 1945 Johannes attended school for the first time in 10 months.

In the midst of his family's flight from danger, Johannes Klaffke dreams of a future as an architect.

Life in the small community remained a challenge. Food was scarce, often just a few bites of bread or a cooked rabbit caught from the forest. Johannes' mother desired to take her family to church, but could not as her children were too weak to make the hour-long trip.

In May 1945 the Germans surrendered to the Allies. The Klaffkes moved from Roringen to Werxhausen where

Johannes continued with his education, rising at 5:00 a.m. each morning to ride in a truck that took him five miles to school on its way to a factory. Each day after school, Johannes and other members of the family worked in fields for which they were paid one mark per day.

> **Each day after school, Johannes and other members of the Klaffke family worked in fields for which they were paid one mark.**

Though his family had no money, Johannes dreamed of a better life, perhaps one in which he might become an architect.

In 1956 at a dance in Osnabruck, Germany, Johannes met a college student named Marianne Niederholtmeyer. Her family, which included seven children, owned farmland and a lumber yard. "Discipline was a part of our lives," she said. "As soon as we arrived home from school, we worked in the garden to ensure we would have food. We also raised chickens and rabbits."

Although the Niederholtmeyers were Catholic, not Jewish, they still lived in fear of the Nazis. One night Marianne and her sister were awakened by shouting on the streets outside their home.

As a school child in Germany, Marianne Niederholtmeyer spends many nights in bomb shelters while learning Hitler's birth date and place of birth at school.

"We knew they were soldiers because we could hear their boot nails against the cobblestones," she said. The commotion lasted a long time. The sisters suspected some of their neighbors may have been arrested and removed from their homes.

Marianne's parents, Heinrich and Agnes Niederholtmeyer, did not believe in Nazi teachings, but kept their thoughts private. "We never talked about what was going on," said Marianne. "We didn't know who in our neighborhood could be trusted."

Many nights the Niederholtmeyer family, hearing the shrill sounds of air raid sirens, ran for safety to shelters. "My sister and I never slept in our pajamas," said Marianne. The shelters, built in the ground, were big enough for 30 people. "We sat with our neighbors until the sirens stopped and the raid was over," she said. "Sometimes we played games through the long hours."

> **At school students like Marianne were required to say, 'Heil Hitler' instead of 'Good morning.'**

At Marianne's school students learned about Hitler, such as where he was born and his birthday. "We were required to say, 'Heil Hitler' instead of 'Good morning'," she said.

Soon after meeting at the dance, Johannes and Marianne fell in love and were married. They desired to start new lives in America.

With the help of sponsors from St. Vincent de Paul Catholic organization in Fort Wayne, the couple immigrated in 1957. Six years later, they were sworn in as American citizens. Johannes and Marianne became parents to four children. They established careers as a cabinet maker and business owner (Johannes) and teacher (Marianne).

The Klaffkes are still active with their community and church. "When we took our citizenship tests, we vowed not to be a burden to the American government," said Johannes. "We're glad we can vote and that it counts."

Roma 'Frankie' Frankland McFarren
Love During War

Sixteen-year-old Roma 'Frankie' Frankland of Melbourne loved to dance, thanks to her three older brothers. "Fred knew the waltz, Vic did a fast jitterbug, and Sid liked the song dances," she said. She was thrilled when they convinced their mother, Evelyn Frankland, to allow Frankie to accompany them to community dances. It was not easy. "Mother thought I'd be kidnapped by white slavers," said Frankie.

Her mother, Evelyn, may not have had as much cause for concern about Frankie being kidnapped at a dance as falling in love.

In September 1939, Australia had declared war on the Axis powers – Germany, Italy, and Japan. As the war progressed, the Red Cross organized dances to entertain the Allied soldiers coming through the country on the way to the Pacific.

The Frankland family meets before Vic leaves for military training. All three Frankland sons will serve in the military and return home. Front: Ernest, Evelyn, Frankie. Back: Vic, Grandpa Trickey, Sid, Fred.

Frankie, whose nickname was given to her by a childhood friend, graduated from McRobertson Girls School, then attended Metropolitan College in 1940. She lived at home while working as a secretary. Frankie's father, Ernest, owned a print shop and Evelyn was a homemaker.

In 1942, American soldiers arrived on the continent as part of the Allies. In Melbourne, the GI's (military lingo for 'government issue') bivouacked in tents at a football field.

As all three of her brothers were in the war, Frankie attended Red Cross dances alone. She was happy to make the soldiers feel welcome, especially Army Private Robert McFarren of Bluffton, Indiana. He was in town on a three-day leave.

Frankie and Robert danced much of their first evening together. "He told me about his duties as an Army photographer," she said. "He was often on the front lines or wherever the action was."

> **During the war, Frankie and Robert wrote letters during months of separation.**

After work each day, Frankie strolled with Robert around Melbourne. "We couldn't go far because we didn't have transportation and couldn't afford the train," she said.

On the third day, Frankie's mother invited Robert to their home for dinner. It was customary for locals to invite soldiers into their homes to eat a home-cooked meal and chat or play board games.

Before parting at the end of the third evening, Frankie and Robert promised to write to each other. The next day when the Army tent city disappeared, Frankie had no idea where Robert had gone or when she might see him again.

The couple wrote letters for nine months. When Robert arranged his leave time to visit Frankie and her family, they rewarded him with another dinner. "Dad even stayed home from the golf course because he liked Robert so much," she said.

Another ten months passed before Frankie and Robert saw each other again. In their correspondence, the couple shared their love for each other. At their next meeting in 1943 they became engaged.

Though Frankie and Robert planned to marry at their next reunion, neither could predict when that might be. This posed a problem with the Church of England where Frankie attended. "I could not get a marriage license ahead of time because a date for the ceremony had to be added," she said. Also, the marital banns had to be read by the minister within three weeks of the marriage.

Frankie had no choice but to pick a date to have the minister read the banns and hope Robert could get there. Somehow, he arrived on time.

On May 6, 1944, Frankie Frankland and Robert McFarren marry in Melbourne, Australia. Frankie lives with her family until the war is over and Robert is discharged. They later moved to America.

On May 6, 1944, the couple was married. As no one from Robert's family was present, Frankie's cousin stood with Robert as his best man. Frankie's parents hired a caterer for the reception held at their home. "I didn't expect them to put so much money into the wedding," she said.

The couple honeymooned at a mountain retreat. As they left the lobby, they met American General Douglas MacArthur. "He and his staff were staying there," said Frankie. The general congratulated the couple on their nuptials.

Frankie stayed with her family while Robert returned to his unit. When the war ended in 1945, she and Robert decided to live in the United States. "He would have stayed in Australia, but I thought he needed to be around family," said Frankie.

In August 1945 she left Australia alone, traveling on a ship with other war brides and staying in Indiana with Robert's family until his discharge. As one of the last group to leave, Robert witnessed the signing of the Tokyo Bay peace treaty.

Robert trained at the New York School of Photography and set up a photography studio with partners in Bluffton. The McFarrens became parents to three children. A son and two grandsons served in the Army. One great-granddaughter is named Sydney after the city in Australia. Robert died in 2001.

For many years Frankie stayed in contact with Leslie, a girlfriend from Australia who had served as her maid of honor. "Leslie married a soldier one week after I did," said Frankie.

General Douglas MacArthur commands the Southwest Pacific during the war. After the war, he will oversee the occupation of Japan.

Robert and Frankie made several trips to Australia to visit with family. "I didn't mind leaving my home and moving to the United States if it meant Bob would be there," she said. "If he had gone to Timbuktu, I would have gone there."

Marigold 'Margot' Wilson McNeely
Bletchley Park, Women's Royal Naval Service (WRN)

Marigold 'Margot' Wilson was 13 years old when war between England and Germany broke out in 1939. Born in London, she lived with her family at Burnham-on-Sea in southwestern England.

In May 1940, Hitler, having already taken over most of Europe, ordered his German Air Force (Luftwaffe) to drop bombs on London and other British cities in an attempt to force Great Britain to surrender.

Although some people believed living in the English countryside during the war was safer than in London, Margot knew otherwise. "Dogfights occurred between English Spitfires and German fighters over our homes," she said. "Shrapnel fell on the roofs."

Margot attended La Retraite Sacred Heart Convent in Somerset. When air-raid alerts sounded, students and staff ran to underground shelters and cellars. "We carried gas masks with us at all times," she said. Fortunately, she never had to use it.

The gas masks provided humor for the students. "It was a challenge not to laugh at the nuns in their black habits teaching while wearing their masks," said Margot.

> **"We students tried not to laugh at the nuns who had to teach while wearing their gas masks," said Margot.**

After graduating from the convent at age 17, Margot volunteered to join the Women's Royal Naval Service (WRNs).

At age 18 English boys and girls were conscripted into service for their country. They could be assigned to the military, factories or farms. "As I had grown up near the seaside, I wanted to be in the Navy," said Margot. Her mother gave her blessing on the choice.

Margot was sent to work at Bletchley Park. The top-secret post an hour north of London was where decoding of enemy messages occurred. Famed mathematician and logician Alan Turing worked on the computer called the Bombe which broke the Nazi Enigma code.

Margot was also assigned to Eastcote, 30 minutes from London on the Underground (tube train). "We worked eight-hour shifts around the clock for a week or ten days before getting leave time," she said. "We had a nice group of girls."

At age 18 Marigold 'Margot' Wilson joins the Women's Royal Naval Service (WRNs). She works at Bletchley Park deciphering codes.

When the WRNs could get away for a break, they often traveled by train to London to attend dances or plays. But the sights weren't always pretty.

Located an hour north of London, Bletchley Park houses the Bombe computer which breaks the Nazi Enigma code during the war.

When Margot and the other WRNs stepped from the train in their Navy uniforms, carrying gas masks, the stench of smoke assailed them. "Hundreds of buildings smoldered from the latest bomb raids," she said. "Sidewalks glistened in the sunlight from shattered glass ground into the cement by the force of bombs."

No matter when air raid sirens wailed, people took cover, usually in the Underground.

Allied military personnel from various countries -- Canada, Australia, Poland, Free French and later, the U.S.
– filled the streets. "They were just about the only people in London," said Margot. A few older men served as firefighters and Home Guard (police). Women volunteered for the Red Cross, Women's Voluntary

Services (WVS) and at canteens, serving sandwiches to the homeless.

No matter when the sirens wailed, day or night, people took cover, usually in the Underground (subway). "We stayed there until the long wail of the 'All Clear' sounded," said Margot. "When we walked out, more buildings were gone."

Early in the war a complete blackout every night over Britain had been instituted. It was hoped the darkness would confuse enemy planes looking for targets. It also made travel for civilians difficult.

> *At night bombs lit London in a ghostly orange glare that silhouetted skeletal ruins of old church spires.*

"Street lights were prohibited due to the blackout," said Margot. "People used torches (flashlights). Every window was boarded up or had blackout curtains. Car headlights were shielded."

The only lights in the skies over London were huge searchlights which crisscrossed looking for enemy planes and incendiary bombs. "At night the bombs lit London in a ghostly orange glare that silhouetted skeletal ruins of old buildings, such as church spires," said Margot.

In early 1944, matters got worse for Londoners. Hitler, having taken a break to send his troops to fight in Russia, returned. Determined to force England to surrender, he ordered V1 and V2 rockets targeted over the English Channel from occupied France.

For Margot, the 'buzz bombs', as they were nicknamed, were the most frightening of all. "They made a screaming noise," she said. "When the noise stopped, we knew they were coming down. We dropped to the ground, covered our heads and hoped for the best. We never knew where they would land." The V1 and V2 were the first rockets used in the war.

When an Enigma operator types the letters of an encrypted letter on this machine, it decodes the secret message.

Following her work in the British naval service and the end of the war, Margot marries an American soldier and moves to America.

"It was a macabre sight," said Margot. "Bombs not only shattered buildings but people and their lives."

Other unusual views were the blimps and barrage balloons hovering overhead. "They were meant to stop Jerry fighter planes from getting too close to a target," she said. "The whole picture of the Blitz is something I will never forget." Note: 'Jerry' was a nickname for the German military.

Yet, as ambulances, police and bomb squads screamed past day and night, Margot and her young friends were not afraid. "We did not think about dying," she said. "We went to military service dances and the Stage Door Canteen and had fun among the ruins."

Margot worked on Turing's Bombe until the war was over. She was discharged in 1947 from HMS Royal Arthur in Corsham Wiltshire. In 1948 she married Captain Richard McNeely, an American Merchant Marine. They moved to America and became parents to four children.

Margot's husband became a ship pilot on the Mississippi River out of New Orleans. The couple raised horses and Great Danes until his death in 2016. Margot has returned to Bletchley Park for reunions, the latest being in 2017.

Today, Margot recalls those chaotic events from decades ago as part of a hazy movie or bad dream. What she has never forgotten is the good that occurred during the war. "The way people pulled together and tried to help one another was wonderful," she said. "It did not matter if we were strangers in a shelter or a bunker. We sat down with cups of tea and became friends. We did not know what the next hour or day would bring. We were bonded in a common cause. That was victory!"

George Rata
Living with the Enemy

By 1945, nine-year-old George Rata no longer flinched at hearing bomb blasts or seeing military planes fly overhead. He had lived at Casa Dorca orphanage in the village of Prilipet, Romania, for three years and he and the other children had grown accustomed to the possibility of an invasion. "We children didn't feel scared," he said. "We knew where to hide."

Leaders at Casa Dorca stocked what little provisions they could spare in the school's basement, planning to hide the orphanage's 42 children there if necessary.

During World War II, the country of Romania sided with the Axis forces from 1941-1944. They then fought with the Allies until the end of the war. No matter whose side the country was for, the Romanians had enemies who drew closer day by day.

With fuel rationed in many Eastern European countries farmers rely on beasts of burden to move goods. Photo by Keith McComb.

George Rata lived at the orphanage, although strictly speaking, he was not an orphan. Born in 1936 in the Romanian village of Resita, he had lost his father to a factory accident in 1942. This left Maria Rata, George's mother, with five children to care for and pregnant with the sixth. George was fourth in line.

To support her family, Maria worked as a custodian in a butcher shop. She taught her children to tend the family's cow, chickens and pigs. The local Baptist church offered additional assistance of food. "I never saw my mother sleep," said George. "She ate what was left after we children were in bed."

In 1942, Maria made the painful decision to send six-year-old George and his four-year-old brother, Dumitru, to Casa Dorca, 60 miles from the Rata home. The other children -- Ion (11), Ana (10), Matei (8) -- were old enough to help Maria at home. A few months later, Maria gave birth to a daughter, Mia.

> **The Germans kept the name of the Casa Dorca orphanage on the front of the building, believing the Allies would not bomb it.**

Casa Dorca was run by a coalition of Baptist churches, providing room, board and education for students between the ages of 3 and 14. As was the case with George and Dumitru, not every child at Casa Dorca was an orphan. "Other students at the orphanage had at least one parent," said George. Poor living conditions covering a wide area necessitated help for families.

Food at the orphanage was simple but adequate -- potato soup and cabbage soup served as staples. Chickens and a cow added additional food as did donations from a Baptist church across the street.

Students at the orphanage were expected to follow rules. "If a student ate an apple from a tree, he or she could be punished," said George. "If our shoes got wet from snow, we may be spanked."

As the war continues, bombed villages become a common site in Europe. Photo by Keith McComb.

The head of the orphanage served as pastor of the Baptist church where the students attended. Youth from the orphanage were required to attend church services three times on Sundays.

"We learned how to sing in a choir and play piano," said George who was also appointed the task of caring for the pastor's cows and chickens at the parsonage two kilometers (approximately 1.3 miles) from the school.

As at the orphanage, rules at the school were strict. "If we did not know our lessons, we would not be served lunch," said George. Between school, church and chores, George and Dumitru stayed busy and spent holidays at the orphanage.

As the war continued into 1945, the orphanage leaders' concern about an invasion came true when German soldiers arrived and took over the building, making it their command center. "The Germans kept the name of the orphanage on the front of the building," said George. "They believed the Allies would not bomb the building if children were inside."

> **For three days, residents of Casa Dorca stayed in the orphanage basement, praying for protection.**

Life became more stressful that spring as rumors spread that the Russian military was headed toward Prilipet. The Germans fled just as the Russians arrived, roaming the village. They looked for German soldiers, vengeful of Romania's allegiance with Germany in the early part of the war.

For three days, the adults and children of Casa Dorca stayed in the orphanage basement, praying the Russians would leave them unharmed.

However, at the village of Bozovici the Russians, still in pursuit of the Germans, were not so lenient. They burned buildings and homes and targeted cannon balls at the church. Villagers tried to put out the fires with bucket brigades, but it was too little, too late.

As a young man, George Rata is thankful to survive childhood and the war.

George was happy to hear his family had escaped danger. "They lived in a village protected by hills and the enemy didn't go there," he said.

Life at the orphanage returned to normal after the Germans and Russians left. However, when the war ended in Europe in May 1945, residents of the village of Prilepet didn't celebrate. "There was always too much work to be done," said George.

When, a year later, Communists took over the orphanage, converting it to a co-op, George, now age 10, returned home to his family. The Rata family now lived in a new home across the street from their old house and George felt happy to be reunited. Dumitru remained at Casa Dorca for another year.

Casa Dorca remained a communist co-op until a revolution in 1989 when it again was free to shelter and care for children in need.

> **After the war, Communists operated Casa Dorca as a co-op until 1989 when it again became an orphanage.**

As an adult, George married and began a family in Romania before deciding to move his family to America. In 1984 he paid a fisherman to take him across the border to Yugoslavia before making his way to the United States.

For two years he worked and saved money for his family to join him. They settled in Los Angeles where George lives today. Maria Rata died in 1980. All of George's siblings are deceased except for his younger sister Mia.

George Rata has returned to Romania several times. The church he attends in Los Angeles sponsors the Casa Dorca orphanage. George's son, Tiberius Rata, a professor at Grace College and Seminary in Indiana, has taken groups of students to visit.

"We didn't think about the war while we were growing up," said George Rata. "We just thought about surviving."

Ursula Dudde Reich
Seeking a New Home

Ursula Dudde's heart pounded as she placed arms around the frightened horse beside her. Despite being harnessed to the family's wagon, the beast nearly pulled the young woman off her feet as it reared, eyes wide with terror.

Feeling his skin tremble beneath her touch, she glanced around. No doubt the sight of falling buildings, bomb blasts and screams of injured people terrorized him as much as it did her.

Ursula had urged her family members to hide in a bomb shelter while she stayed on the street with the horse. Ursula knew aircraft strafing the area was both Russian and American. She wanted nothing more than to bury her face in the steed's furry neck to block out the terror. There was no safe place to hide!

Born in 1923 in Darkehmen, a province of East Prussia (today the area is Ozyorsk in Russia), Ursula became accustomed to hard work. Her father, Otto, was a farmer in charge of four families who lived and worked on the Dudde property.

Farmers in Eastern Europe pool resources and manpower to accomplish tasks like threshing. Photo by Charles Dunwoody.

This was a common occurrence in the feudal system practiced by farmers in the area. Men worked in the fields and with livestock, while women cooked, cleaned, kept house, gardened and supervised children. A family graveyard on the property attested to the Dudde's presence there for 300 years.

Like many families in wartime Europe, the Duddes had suffered many losses. Ursula's fiancé, Kurt Reich, had been killed when German troops invaded Russia.

Ursula's father died at home. An older brother, Otto, died during the war while fighting in Crete. Another brother,

Kurt, went to war but never came home. Ursula believed he may have been captured by the Russians and put to death in a Siberian prison.

In 1944, having heard the Russian army was drawing near to their home, Ursula knew her family was in danger.

After enduring years of oppression by the Germans including the murders of millions of its citizens, Russia's Red Army was set on vengeance. If caught, German civilians believed they would not be taken prisoner but killed. Ursula had to save her family.

German troops killing millions of people while fighting in Russia in 1941.

Ursula worked as a teacher and was good at organizing people. She helped her mother, Bertha, 12-year-old brother, female friend and a Polish farm worker quickly load their belongings on a wagon. The group headed west with no destination in mind. Anywhere safe from the Russians would suit them.

During the winter of 1944 and 1945, record-low temperatures made life on the road for Ursula's group challenging. Ditches along the road and an occasional hog house with straw for warmth provided protection from the cold.

During their travels, Ursula and her family witnessed horrifying sights, including ditches full of dead bodies with no one to bury them.

Upon entering yet another city, Ursula watched, horrified, as bombs descended and buildings collapsed. 'I hope the next bomb hits me,' she thought in despair. 'I just want it to be over.' For her family's sake, Ursula tried to focus on settling the horse and securing what remained of her family's belongings in the wagon.

> **For the rest of her life Ursula would never forget what it was like to be hungry.**

By sheer will, her family arrived in western Germany, settling at a refugee camp where they felt safe. Food was in notoriously short supply during the remainder of the war and for several years afterward. For the rest of her life Ursula would remember what it was like to be hungry and never complaining about anything she ate.

Life took a turn for the better when in 1948 Ursula married Bruno Reich, Kurt's brother. Bruno had been a paratrooper in the German military. The couple became parents to two sons, Hans and Dieter.

One of Bruno's uncles had immigrated to America. He lived in a small town in northeast Indiana called Bluffton and encouraged Bruno and Ursula to move there with their sons. After their application for emigration was accepted, the Reichs left Germany in 1953 with little more than a set of clothes.

The Reichs worked for a local farmer before eventually purchasing a 60-acre farm. For four decades the Reichs worked the land, raised grain and cared for a variety of livestock, including dairy and beef cattle, pigs, geese, chickens, and veal calves.

In 1984 Bruno died following a heart attack. More sorrow for Ursula followed in 1997 when Dieter died from a farm accident.

A few years prior to her death in 2012, a counselor diagnosed Ursula with post-traumatic stress syndrome. "He said as a civilian she suffered the same symptoms of war that a soldier would have," said Hans Reich.

Despite her prayer for her life to end during the war and the struggles she encountered later in life, Ursula was the last member of her original family to survive, a testament to her strong will and ultimate belief that life was indeed worth living.

Charlotte Butterfield Schnieders
Attack at Pearl Harbor

Shortly before 8:00 a.m. on Sunday, December 7, 1941, hundreds of Japanese aircraft conducted a surprise blitz on the American Naval Fleet stationed at Pearl Harbor at Hawaii. By 10:00 a.m. much of the fleet was destroyed or seriously damaged.

Seven American battleships were sunk or too crippled to be of use. One of the sunken ships included the USS Arizona, which lost 1,177 crew members.

The total number of military personnel killed at Pearl Harbor was 2,335, including 68 civilians injured or killed as a result of the attack.

The assault at Pearl Harbor was part of a plan to eliminate America's potential challenge to Japanese control in Asia. The incident represents the U.S. Navy's greatest disaster.

**

On the morning of December 7, 1941, Lillian Butterfield, 27, received a phone call at her home in downtown Honolulu. As it was her day off at Queen's Medical Center (then Queen's Hospital), she was surprised to be asked to report for work.

The hospital staff person offered no explanation as to why Lillian was being asked to report for duty. All she said was that the same request was being made of all off-duty nursing staff.

The USS *Arizona* is one of several American ships that burns as a result of the Japanese attack on Pearl Harbor.

Lillian didn't question the request for help. Any time she could provide nursing care to people in need, she was willing.

At about the same time Lillian's husband, George Butterfield, received a similar call for help from his supervisor at Hickam Field.

> **During the attack, Japanese fighters bombed Hickam Field's flight line and hangars where dozens of planes were parked.**

The military base had been established in 1935 as Hawaii's principal army airfield and bomber base. George Butterfield worked as a civilian machinist. Like his wife, George agreed to give up his free time for the as-yet unknown emergency.

Lillian and George had met when George's family moved to Hawaii a few years earlier. Lillian was born in Hawaii following her grandparents settling there from Portugal to work in Hawaii's sugarcane fields.

Note: At the time of the attack on Pearl Harbor the series of islands in the South Pacific called Hawaii was a United States territory. After a two-year period of annexation, the territory was granted statehood along with Alaska in 1959 with Hawaii being declared the 50th state to be added to the Union.

Lillian took her and George's only child, two-year-old Charlotte, from their home near Diamondhead to Lillian's parents' house on the other side of the island at Kailua Beach. Lillian's father worked for the Hawaiian Parks Department at Kailua Beach.

Charlotte's grandparents soon discovered via neighbors the cause for their sudden opportunity to babysit -- the Japanese military had attacked Pearl Harbor early that morning.

The result of the attack was devastating. While primarily targeting battleships and carriers, Japanese fighters and dive-bombers had strafed and bombed the flight line and hangars at Hickam Field where dozens of planes sat on the ground.

For years after the attack, Lillian Butterfield has nightmares of images of planes flying low over Hawaii.

Nearly half of the airplanes at Hickam Field were destroyed or severely damaged. The Hawaiian Air Depot, base fire station, chapel and guardhouse had all been hit and thousands of people killed, including civilians.

The second wave of the Japanese attack struck Hickam at 8:40 a.m. By 9:45 a.m., the attacks were over and the Japanese pilots gone. The surprise attack by the Japanese had far-reaching effects for the citizens of Hawaii. Within hours of the attack, Territorial Governor Joseph Poindexter placed Hawaii under martial law. Every person living in Hawaii was fingerprinted including infants. Citizens over the age of seven were issued an official identification card which had to be carried at all times.

> *Under martial law food on Hawaii was rationed and liquor banned. Luxury hotels housed military personnel.*

Rather than cards, younger children were issued bracelets with an attached disc that carried their identification information. "My bracelet contained my first and last names, blood type, and assigned identification number," said Charlotte.

She was too young to wear one of the gas masks issued to all Hawaiian civilians over the age of seven. The masks were to prepare for the possibility of poison gas attacks or air raids.

Fearing they could be attacked again, the Hawaiians lived under a nightly blackout rule, which was strictly enforced. Every building's windows were draped and every street light darkened and vehicle headlights covered. The efforts to prevent the enemy from viewing potential targets continued through most of the duration of the war.

Barbed wire was placed around beaches, water pumping stations, electrical installations and government buildings. Civilians dug holes for bomb shelters and many private homes and public places prepared to house people during a raid.

Following the attack, young children are issued bracelets with an attached identification disc.

Food on the island was rationed and liquor banned. Luxury hotels, devoid of tourists, housed military personnel. No photos of the islands were permitted to be taken and if cameras were found, they were confiscated.

Days passed before Lillian Butterfield was granted a break to return to her home and family. Though her hospital was not on a military base, it was used to assist in the injuries incurred from the attack. "The nurses were kept very busy at that time," said Charlotte.

George maintained long hours repairing damaged equipment from the bombs and strafing. "Dad's job was to get things back to normal so we islanders could defend ourselves," said Charlotte.

But the people of Hawaii did not want to be seen as victims. During the next few months, they performed a number of tasks to ensure their safety and to show they would never again be an easy target. One of these was when the Army tested and refined a special weapon called a flame thrower. These were frequently used in the Pacific campaigns against the enemy entrenched in bunkers and pill boxes.

Due to the need for females to participate in essential war work in the islands, Hawaii's women were not allowed to enlist until October 1944. Then the 59 women who did join were sent to Fort Oglethorpe in Georgia for basic training, then on to specialty schools including Fort Des Moines in Iowa.

Following the news of Japan's surrender in September 1945, the people of Hawaii grew immeasurably during the war years. Racial, cultural and economic barriers were breached, while improved air transportation made easier access to the islands. Tourism flourished with the growth of hotels, restaurants and entertainment venues.

But not every resident benefited from the war. For Charlotte Butterfield the attack at Pearl Harbor caused her to suffer from nightmares for years. "Though I was a young child during the assault on Pearl Harbor, I dreamed about seeing planes fly over our house and was terrified," she said. The dreams continued for many years.

Charlotte lived in Hawaii until graduating from high school. She moved to the mainland to attend Chatham College in Pittsburgh, Pennsylvania to work on a degree in Oriental Art History. She returned to the islands, finishing her education at the University of Hawaii.

While attending church in Honolulu, Charlotte met John Lawrence Schnieders of Fort Wayne, Indiana. John had enlisted in the U.S. Navy and served four years active duty and four years in the Reserves before being discharged.

In 1960 John and Charlotte married in Honolulu before moving to Fort Wayne, where John worked in the computer industry. They became parents to five children.

Eileen 'Lynne' Welch Shanahan
Bomb Survivor

In fall 1940, Alfred Welch and his wife Violet wanted to celebrate the grand opening of their butcher shop happening the next day. At that time residents of London didn't have much cause for celebration. Nearly every night the German Air Force dropped bombs on the city and other parts of England in an attempt to force the British people to surrender. Despite the devastation and thousands of deaths, the people of Great Britain continued to resist Hitler's aggression.

Before leaving that evening for the pub (restaurant) down the street, the Welches carefully placed their children – four-year-old Eileen ('Lynne'); two-year-old twins Pamela and Anthony and infant Barbara -- in an underground bunker in the backyard garden. Bunkers were a common sight in Camberwell, the section of south London where the Welches lived. The shelters provided safety during bomb raids with enough room for a family to sit up or sleep through the night.

Following a bombing on their London home, Lynne Welch (back row, left) and siblings leave the city, never to return.

The parents had not been gone long when 'Jerry' arrived.('Jerry' was a nickname the Allies gave to the German military).

Among the dozens of incendiary bombs that dropped on the city that night was one that flattened the Welches' flat (apartment) above their butcher shop. Rubble from the explosion spewed over the bunker, trapping the children inside.

The Welches hurried home to find neighbors pulling the four Welch children from the destroyed bunker. Amazingly, none were harmed. "We children were not scared," said Lynne. "We did not understand what had happened and thought it was an adventure."

The damage to their home and near deaths of their children caused Violet and Alfred to made quick decisions. Within 24 hours Violet and all of the children were on a train headed south toward Cornwall. They had joined Operation Pied Piper.

Children sit outside the remainder of their London home, the result of another Nazi bombing raid in fall 1940.

In an effort to save children living in cities under attack during what became known as the 'Blitz' the British government devised an organized plan of evacuation. During Operation Pied Piper, registered children were relocated away from London to areas throughout the British Isles thought to be safe.

The Welches were assigned to a farm family in Cornwall. Violet and the children were given one room to live in. They prepared and ate their meals separately as the farmer and his wife preferred to keep to themselves.

Not everyone in Cornwall seemed reluctant to meet the newcomers. The farmer's two young daughters were eager to make friends. "I think we were someone new for them to play with," said Lynne.

> **When Violet Welch learned someone didn't have enough food stamps, she offered her own.**

With his family and butcher shop gone, Alfred found somewhere to live and employment with another butcher. Each weekend he rode the train to Cornwall to visit his family, taking funds from his earnings to share with them.

The Welches were helped with provisions via ration books. Every British citizen, including children, was issued one filled with stamps (coupons) for food and clothing.

Despite the daily struggle to provide food for her family, Violet never hesitated to show generosity to others. "One day we were in the shops and Mum heard someone say they didn't have enough food stamps," said Lynne. "Mum offered some of her own." The Welch family, in turn, was aided by local farmers who shared apples from their harvest.

Army soldiers help children living in the midst of war by offering candy and companionship. Photo courtesy Dennis Butler (pictured above).

Four months after moving out of London, Violet moved her children from the farm to an abandoned railroad car. Converted to living quarters with the barest of necessities -- wood stove, sink, and oven – the car was tight on space but offered one thing the farm lacked -- privacy.

The Welches quickly adjusted to their new digs. After carrying buckets of water from a well each morning for their needs, Lynne attended school, making friends and doing well in her studies.

In 1943 Violet delivered another set of twins – boys named Malcolm and Douglas. Each week Violet loaded a pram (baby carriage) with four of her children to walk four miles to the village of Launceston to shop. Lynne and one of the older children walked alongside.

> *American soldiers delivered boxes of food and a wireless (radio) to the delight of the Welch family.*

One day the Welches met American soldiers on the road. The soldiers, training in the area for battle, stopped to chat with Violet and the children. "They were astounded at seeing our two sets of twins," said Lynne. From then on, the soldiers delivered boxes of food to the Welch family.

On one occasion the soldiers delivered a special gift. "They carried a box with a lady singing inside," said Lynne. It was a wireless, or radio -- the first one the Welches had seen. Violet and the children were delighted.

At Christmas Violet prepared a special meal for the soldiers, serving mincemeat pie. It was a cozy time, especially when one soldier shared a photo of his young son. When Alfred arrived, he cried. "Dad knew those young men had helped us survive," said Lynne.

Weeks later, the Welches and other people in the area watched the soldiers leave to fight in Europe. "They marched through town singing 'Lily by the Lamplight'," said Lynne. "We never saw them again."

> *"Dad was grateful the American soldiers had helped us survive," said Lynne.*

In 1943 Alfred moved his family to a new place in Dorset. The thatched roof cottage contained two rooms, but Violet made a comfortable home. A religious woman, Violet took her children to church each Sunday and earned money by cleaning houses during the week.

By the time the war ended in 1945, the Welches had decided to remain in the south. Lynne finished school a few years later and, having shown talent as a dancer, joined an acrobatic troupe traveling to Cypress, Iran, and Athens. Upon moving to California, Lynne became a nanny for Hollywood actor William Conrad. In 1981 she married Robert Shanahan, an American Marine. Robert is deceased.

Lynne keeps in contact with friends and family members in England and around the world. She attends church, helps homeless veterans and recalls the example set by her mother. "Mum had it difficult during the war because she had so much to do," she said. "She set a good example for giving love to others."

Mary Lou Bowers Smith
Civil Air Patrol

On Sunday, December 7, 1941, 13-year-old Mary Lou Bowers and her family attended services at St. Mary's Catholic Church in Huntington, Indiana. After lunch, they drove to the country, intending to spend a leisurely afternoon riding in their car. They had only driven a short time when an announcement on the radio was made that would change their lives and the lives of millions of people around the world.

Upon hearing the startling news that the Japanese military had attacked Pearl Harbor in Hawaii, Mary Lou's father turned the car around. "We wanted to get home to listen on our big Philco radio about the attack," she said.

Being entertained while listening to the radio was a nightly event in the Bowers home. Harry and Bertha 'Bird' – Mary Lou's parents -- enjoyed comedy shows like *Amos and Andy* and *The Jack Benny Show*.

That nigh regular programming was interrupted by President Franklin D. Roosevelt. "He said our country was possibly going to war," said Mary Lou.

... we here highly resolve that these dead shall not have died in vain ...

REMEMBER DEC. 7th!

Patriotic posters create a link to the Homefront and military front lines.

Although too young to understand everything President Roosevelt said, Mary Lou, 14, knew it was serious situation.

She was the third of four children in the Bowers family. Before the Depression forced its closure, Harry had owned a motorcycle shop in Wabash, 30 miles from Huntington. Afterward, Harry worked any job he could find before securing employment with the Erie Railroad as a conductor.

The Bowers family showed support for the war by Bird working for the war bond board. The war became more real when Mary Lou's older brother, Ralph, was drafted into the Navy.

Adults and children present ration books filled with coupons to grocers and stores for food and clothing.

Mary Lou, like most people, discovered ways to help the war effort. As many foods were suddenly rationed, people were encouraged to plant seeds to help feed the nation. These plots became known as Victory Gardens.

The Bowers family had never planted a garden, but Mary Lou didn't let that stop her. When a neighbor offered a small plot of land a couple of blocks from her home, she accepted.

With many foods rationed, Americans were encouraged to plant Victory Gardens to help feed the nation.

The teen who had never held a spade took on the project with gusto. That spring, when the weather got warmer, she tilled the soil each day after school to prepare it for planting. Later, she dropped in seeds issued to her and other gardeners by the county extension agent. Corn, beans, cabbage, lettuce, carrots – anything she could get to grow became a challenge to Mary Lou.

The efforts of her and other Victory Gardeners did not go unnoticed. When the town of Huntington awarded prizes to the people who grew the biggest vegetables, Mary Lou won a $25 war bond for the produce in her garden.

Inspired by her success for the war effort, Mary Lou took her patriotism one step further. In early 1942 an adult neighbor encouraged her to join a new group called Civil Air Patrol (CAP). Although Mary Lou didn't know much about the national group, other than that it was being formed to help with the war effort, she decided to join.

"I've always liked learning new things," she said. The goal of CAP was to help the nation's defense. "We were taught cloud formations, military drills, how to identify allied and enemy aircraft and weather conditions," said Mary Lou. The group was assigned the number 523.

"In Civil Air Patrol we learned cloud formations, military drills, how to identify enemy aircraft and weather conditions," said Mary Lou.

Among the approximately 20 members of the CAP were a dozen or so teenage girls. Mary Lou's parents approved of their daughter's involvement in the group. In fact, Bird Bowers may have had personal reasons for encouraging her daughter to stretch societal boundaries. In the 1930s when the majority of women wore dresses or skirts, Bird had donned pants to ride motorcycles from her husband's shop.

The half dozen students between the ages of 14-18 who joined CAP did not have to pay dues to join the group, but they did have to commit to attending weekly meetings year-round. In later years, cadets, as the students were called, would be issued uniforms. At the beginning of the war the organization was more informal with no uniforms and policies, practices and protocol that were established.

When not involved with CAP, Mary Lou plays in her school's band. Music becomes a major part of her young life.

It was exciting for Mary Lou, especially as she occasionally had the opportunity to accompany adult leaders during flights in small planes. "I thought flying was great fun," she said.

Students around the nation also discovered the excitement of the group. CAP volunteers guarded all civilian airports. The hunt for scrap materials incited a group to discover an abandoned bridge and old schoolhouse bells that could be used for vitally needed brass and bronze.

> *"I was proud of what we in CAP did for our country," said Mary Lou. "It made me want to be a better citizen."*

Another group of CAP members along the East Coast spotted enemy submarines, thus aiding the military troops in that area.

But ultimately, CAP was not as influential in Mary Lou's life as another passion – music. In the fifth grade her talent had been good enough for her to play the oboe with the Huntington High School band. As a sophomore, she accompanied the Fort Wayne Symphony, making her the youngest member to join the group.

Due to the intense time needed to practice, Mary Lou eventually had to choose between CAP and music. The possibility of making the latter a career became the deciding factor.

Turning down a full-ride scholarship to Indiana University after graduating in 1945, she moved to Chicago to play for the symphony there. Mary Lou later married an army veteran named Don Smith. Together, they worked for a musical instrument company, while also raising four children.

When she was in her 40s, Mary Lou attended college, earning two bachelor and two master's degrees. She became a representative for the American Institute for Foreign Study, accompanying groups of students to Europe. In the 1970s, Cambridge University in England presented Mary Lou with its "International Woman of the Year" award.

Today, Mary Lou Bowers Smith attributes much of her success in life to her involvement with CAP. "I was proud of what we did for our country," she said. "It made me feel of value and want to be a better citizen."

Margie Stewart
Official Poster Girl of the U.S. Army

During World War II, millions of GIs had her face pasted above their beds. Nearly all knew her by her first name. At the height of her popularity 94 million posters with her photo were printed and distributed to American servicemen.

Yet today few people are aware of the young woman who achieved the unique status as the only official poster girl of the U.S. Army.

Margie Stewart was born in Wabash, Indiana, in 1919. An active student at Wabash High School, she participated in the Girls Athletic Association, Science Club, Dramatic Club, yearbook staff, and as a cheerleader ('yell leader').

After graduating in 1937, Margie attended Indiana University in Bloomington. She was judged the campus' most popular freshman co-ed in a contest. Her prize included a summer trip to Chicago where, after quitting school, Margie found employment as a model for an advertising agency. A similar type of job at a women's department store earned her $24 a week.

"Please don't gamble [ ] [ ] with your LIFE!"

BE CAREFUL WHAT YOU SAY or write!

Margie Stewart works as a department store model and film actress before posing for the military.

In 1941 Margie moved to Los Angeles to further her modeling work. She found a job in another major department store, but Margie had more goals for her life than to be peered at by shoppers amongst racks of clothes. When RKO Pictures offered her a trial contract and pay of $75 a week, she accepted.

The first movie Margie appeared in was 1942's 'Here We Go Again.' The following year she appeared in 'Bombardier', a film starring Pat O'Brien, Randolph Scott and Ann Shirley. Louella Parsons, motion picture editor of the International News Service, described Margie as a 'vivacious newcomer to the screen'. Margie was later cast in small parts in more than a dozen movies.

While working as a starlet, Margie volunteered at the Hollywood Canteen, a place for Allied service people to eat. The club, organized by Hollywood actors Bette Davis and John Garfield, was run by volunteers in the film and entertainment industry, providing free food, dancing and entertainment to servicemen waiting to be shipped overseas.

Stage Door Canteens around the United States are run by volunteers in the film and entertainment industry, offering food, entertainment and socializing to troops.

At the Canteen Margie waited on tables, cooked in the kitchen and helped with clean up. She also talked and danced with GIs, attempting to calm their fears before they were shipped out.

Throughout the war, Margie participated in hospital tours with the USO in California, Texas, New Mexico, Oregon, and Washington to raise the morale of sick and wounded soldiers. During this time, she appeared in several war time instructional videos.

> *In an attempt to boost morale among troops, American military officials produced posters featuring Margie Stewart.*

However, not even the best publicity agent could have anticipated Margie's skyrocketing popularity with the military posters flaunting her girl-next-door attraction.

In an attempt to boost morale among troops, military officials came up with the idea of producing posters featuring one female who showed support for the war. Having seen Margie in films and print ads, they asked her to pose to remind troops of the people at home wishing them well.

Margie was not the typical pin-up model. Compared to the 1943 publicity shot of swimsuit-clad Betty Grable peeking coquettishly over her shoulder, Margie appeared modestly dressed in the posters, giving her the image for many GIs of girls they had grown up with.

So many troops show interest in Margie Stewart that her pictures are printed on service men's paychecks.

American soldiers thought of the blue-eyed brunette as the sweetheart awaiting them at home (or wishing she was).

When her wide eyes looked imploringly at the camera above the printed words 'Please get there and back', a sailor felt obliged to obey. Her look of concern on the poster stating 'Be careful what you say or write' went straight to the heart of airmen flying in the South Pacific and Europe.

Her admonition to soldiers to buy war bonds for a brighter future after the war encouraged Army troops to invest their money.

Troop response to the Margie Posters was robust. So many troops showed interest in the young woman that Stewart was asked to pose for 12 more posters. Her pictures were even printed on service men's paychecks.

> **First Lady Eleanor Roosevelt's removal of Margie's posters caused troops to protest. The posters were put back into circulation.**

One prominent person objected to Margie's popularity and nearly put an end to the posters.

First Lady Eleanor Roosevelt believed the posters would make GIs homesick. When she petitioned to stop the printing and distribution of the posters, so many letters poured in from troops in protest that the order was rescinded. Stewart's posters were put back in circulation.

Despite her fame, Margie did not forget her hometown. During the war, she visited Wabash to help with the war bond drive, participating in Bingo games and chatting with girlfriends from school and other friends and being photographed for the newspaper.

Her work for the war effort did not end after Germany's surrender in May 1945. One month later, she received an official request from General Dwight D. Eisenhower. He had served as Supreme Commander of the Allied Forces in Europe for D-Day in June 1944. Eisenhower would later be voted as the United States President.

When Eisenhower asked Margie to go to Europe to help with 7th War Loan Bond Drive, she agreed. In June 1945

WABASH FINDS WAY TO SELL BON

Movie starlet Margie Stewart came back to her home town, Wabash, Ind., recently to help boost the sale of war bonds and stamps. The entire town co-operated in the effort, which resulted in the sale of $25,000 worth of bonds. Prizes were given for most attractive war bond booths of merchants in the city. A booster breakfast and a big program at the Armory in the evening were features of the event.—Wabash Camera Club Photos.

During a visit to Wabash, Margie is photographed for the local newspaper.

Margie traveled to Europe, visiting troops in France and London. Upon learning of her scheduled appearance at Hyde Park, the staff at *Stars & Stripes*, a military magazine, promoted her tour.

Margie visited airfields, shops, and offices, posing for pictures and eating beans at an enlisted men's mess, all the while signing autographs. The trip became extra special as in Paris, Margie was introduced to Captain Jerry Johnson, head of the Entertainment Division for Allied Forces. After a brief courtship, the couple married before she resumed her list of scheduled visits in Europe.

The news of Margie Stewart's marriage made news. Editors of *Stars & Stripes* printed the headline that presumably echoed the lament of every GI: 'Margie, How Could You?'

After her stint in Europe was completed, Margie and her husband returned to southern California where they became producers for the Hollywood Bowl. They were parents to one son and celebrated more than 50 years together before Jerry died in 2003.

> **The wholesome image of Margie Stewart on posters was designed to remind troops of friends and families who awaited them at home.**

Beginning in 1972 Margie volunteered at UCLA Center for Health. For several years she offered comfort to families, registering patients, delivering mail and newspapers. By the end of her volunteering career, she had given 3,850 hours of time. Margie Stewart Johnson died from symptoms of pneumonia in 2012.

Although Margie never had a major role in films, she played a significant part in reminding soldiers, sailors and airmen of the friends and families who awaited them at home. A display of some of the Army's official pin-up girl's personal items is on display at the Wabash County History Museum in Wabash, Indiana.

Berenice Everett Stoppenhagen
A Home in Wales

Berenice Everett ran through the streets of south London as fast as her short legs would carry her. As on many nights, Berenice's parents had dragged their six children from their beds during yet another bombing raid. Though Berenice was not yet in school, she knew every minute counted before reaching the underground shelter.

Inside, the Everett family huddled, surrounded by friends and neighbors. As the nightly raids continued, the atmosphere within the air raid shelters became friendly. "People sang to pass the time," said Berenice. "Many left bedrolls and mattresses because they knew they would mostly likely return the following night."

The Everett family is one of thousands divided when British children are sent away from cities for protection as part of Operation Pied Piper. Front, L-R: Berenice, Janet, John. Back, L-R: Maureen, mother Emily, Violet. Brother Victor is in the hospital. Sister Lynn is born later.

Berenice was the third of seven children born to Herbert and Emily Everett. When England declared war against Germany in September 1939, Herbert was conscripted as a cook for the British Army on the Isle of Wight, off the south coast of England.

"The only times we children saw our father until the war ended in 1945 was when he came home for an occasional leave," said Berenice.

> **At one point young Berenice, terrorized by the air raids, refused to go to the bomb shelter. "I hid under a table," she said.**

From September 1940 through May 1941, Hitler's Luftwaffe (Air Force) performed bombing raids on parts of England. The British people endured destruction, strict rationings and loss of life, yet they remained valiant in their determination not to be conquered. "Our family moved three times because each house we lived in was destroyed," said Berenice.

Despite their courage, the onslaught of deadly aggression was a frightening time, especially for children. At one point Berenice became so terrorized she hid under the family's kitchen table. "I refused to go to the bomb shelter," she said.

With the deaths of thousands of British people and daily upheaval in cities along the coast, an organized effort was made to secure the English children's welfare by evacuating them to locations further inland. The plan was called Operation Pied Piper.

An aircraft spotter on a building in London looks for Luftwaffe (German planes) over St. Paul's Cathedral and other buildings.

At age three, Berenice was evacuated with sisters Violet, 7, and Maureen, 6. The younger Everett children remained in London with their mother.

The trio boarded a train in London along with dozens of other children, each carrying gas masks and ration books. "Mum tucked my train ticket into my coat to make sure I didn't lose it," said Berenice. After a child was assigned to a home, his or her parents would receive the contact information.

At towns all across England the children were paraded before villagers who chose which ones they wanted to live with them. The train took the Everett sisters to Wales.

Perhaps it was the strain of being away from home or the weariness of travel. For whatever reason, at the Welsh village of Glamorgan little Berenice began to cry.

> *Emily Everett rode the train monthly to Wales to visit her daughters, accompanied by their baby brother.*

A teenage girl spotted Berenice. She may have taken pity on the sisters for she led them to a big house nestled in the mountains. The teen's father, a tailor, and his wife made the girls feel welcome to their home which to the girls' delight housed the family's cat.

Only later would Berenice and her sisters discover the tailor's wife had wanted her daughter to bring home a boy to help around the home. Still, the new guests were treated as members of the family for the several months they resided there (Berenice cannot recall their names).

When Violet and Maureen attended school, Berenice did too. "We liked it and did well," she said. At home the girls completed chores, including working in the garden. On Sundays they attended services at the Church of England with their host family. "The church singing was wonderful," she added.

Once a month Emily Everett traveled by train to visit her daughters, accompanied by their new baby brother, John. As the bombings dragged on, the reunions became more poignant. One Christmas Berenice, having been chosen as the fairy at the top of the Christmas tree for a school play, looked down from her perch. Spying her mother, she cried with gladness. "They had to get me down," she said.

Signs of devastation are evident throughout London and other places in Europe. Photo by Charles Dunwoody.

By the time, the sisters returned to London after the bombings stopped in 1944, Berenice only knew the Welsh language.

The announcement of the end of the war in Europe on May 8, 1945 (VE Day 'Victory in Europe'), was cause for celebration. "Food had been scarce during the war," said Berenice. "People shared what they had on tables in the streets. It was a big party!"

Berenice attended Silverthorn School for Girls until the standard age of 15, then worked in a law court as a clerk.

In 1962, she and a girlfriend moved to America, finding jobs as secretaries in Fort Wayne, Indiana.

Berenice worked for two years before marrying Raymond Stoppenhagen, a farmer from Ossian, Indiana. They became parents to four children. Berenice worked as a licensed practical nurse for many years.

After Raymond's death in 1995, Maureen, who had lived in New York City, moved in with Berenice. She died in 2009. Violet is also deceased. Berenice keeps in touch with the younger Everett siblings in England.

"I pray my grandchildren never have to see a war like what we lived through," said Berenice. "I wish people could talk better instead of fighting."

Marie Libersa Vance
French Resistance Worker

Marie Louise Libersa knew her parents had high hopes for her. As Dr. Gaston Libersa and his wife, Mathilde, had instilled a desire to achieve in each of their seven children four became doctors. They believed Marie could become a pharmacist.

No doubt the young woman raised near Faverney in the Haute-Saone region in Eastern France was intelligent. Marie had graduated from college in Paris in 1942. She hoped to find work as a teacher.

But Marie had other plans for her life right then. She wanted to help her country in its time of desperate need.

Since the summer of 1940, France had been under the control of Nazi Germany. Poland, Greece, Netherlands, Belgium, Norway, Luxembourg, Denmark, and Yugoslavia had also fallen in defeat.

The French people hated Hitler's domination and his German soldiers who forced their way into homes and businesses, demanding food and supplies. The French people longed to have their freedoms restored.

> ***Marie's work in the Resistance included using her skills with French, English, German and Arabic languages.***

The answer for Marie came in the form of an invitation – would she serve as an interpreter for the French Underground?

Marie was not only fluent in French, English, and German but Arabic, a language taught to her by her father. Language skills were useful in the Underground, especially as Arab-speaking people were part of the French army.

Gaston, a veterinarian, had already joined the French army to care for horses used by the cavalry. He had early on recognized Marie's adventurous spirit. "He always called me 'Nosy' because I was curious about things," she said.

During the next few years, Marie was one of a handful of women who served as interpreters for the French Resistance. These small groups of men and women obtained information about the Germany military, passing it on to the Allies. They also maintained escape routes for downed Allied soldiers and airmen trapped behind enemy lines. If caught, their lives would have been lost, as well as those they helped.

An American officer and French partisan (Resistance worker) crouch behind an auto during a street fight in a French city, ca. 1944

Much of Marie's time was spent interpreting for German prisoners of war during interrogations. Sometimes it was difficult to maintain an emotional distance, especially near the end of the war when the German army consisted of mostly young boys.

Marie recalled one teen who was homesick. "He started crying so I sang a lullaby," she said. "He said it was like one his mother had sung."

During her work with the French Resistance, Marie interprets for French General Charles de Gaulle, seen here speaking at Cherbourg in 1944.

Marie adapted new skills, which included parachuting out of planes, something she did on three occasions. "I was needed at places like Spain and traveling by plane was the only way to get there," she said. "I thought it was fun and never felt my life was danger."

During the course of her duties, Marie interpreted for Charles de Gaulle. The French Army officer led one of the few successful military operations against Germany during the initial invasion of France. He became the unofficial leader of the Free French and Resistance forces, groups essential in preparation for the landings at Normandy in June 1944. In the 1950s, de Gaulle would be elected President of France.

In this poster French people are urged to maintain a spirit of dissatisfaction while under the domination of the German government.

Marie was not intimidated by the statesman's presence. "He was polite, serious and careful of what he said," she said.

Despite living in stressful circumstances, Marie never became sick or was injured. She always had enough food to eat. The American military paid her for her work with the French underground. "I didn't get much money," she said, "but I had everything I needed, which was food, clothing, and a place to sleep. I felt proud of what I was doing. I had a high security rating. The soldiers respected me and my work."

As a young woman, Marie Libersa Vance sets aside her dreams of teaching to help the French Resistance. Later, she will take on a new adventure with an American husband in America.

When American troops arrived in Europe to aid the Allies, Marie attended dances organized for them. In 1945, she met Glenn Vance, a native of Fort Wayne, Indiana. When he asked Marie to dance, she agreed.

As part of the American Infantry, Glenn Vance had been injured at the Battle of the Bulge in early 1945 and evaded capture by pretending to be dead. At the dance he shared with Marie that he was convalescing for an injury to his ankle.

The couple fell in love, but it was a tricky courtship. "Glenn didn't always know where I was and I didn't know where he was," she said. "One has no idea what war is like until one is in it."

The couple married in 1946 after the war ended by a Justice of the Peace in Reims, France. The only family member present was Marie's mother.

The Vances planned to move to America. Knowing Glenn would soon be discharged, Marie left her native country for the United States.

After disembarking at New York City, she traveled by train to Fort Wayne, renting an apartment for the two of them and hiring out as an interpreter. "Lots of refugees were arriving in the city at that time," she said.

Glenn arrived a few months later and found work at Zollner, a piston factory, in Fort Wayne. Marie became a teacher. The couple became parents to six children. Glenn is deceased.

"I was proud and glad to have been a part of World War II," said Marie. "Dad may have been disappointed I did not go into the medical field, but during the war he wrote me a letter and told me he was proud of me. He let me know I may not have been official like a soldier, but I helped."

Discussion Questions

1. Compare lifestyles during the war of American children with those born in Europe. Who had it easier? Why?

2. What alternatives might the British people have had to sending children to live with strangers to keep them safe?

3. How did the youth like Alex Jokay maintain a positive view of life while scared, starving and trying to escape the enemy?

4. What part did religious faith play in the lives of these families?

5. What might the parents of children sent away, either for protection or military service, have felt?

6. How might the Jacksons' lives have been different if Gerald's memory had not been restored?

7. What other jobs besides working in war material factories did American women perform to help the war effort?

8. Why did the youth living in Europe decide as adults to move to the United States?

9. What do you think the author's purpose was in writing this book? What ideas was she trying to get across?

10. What have these stories taught you about facing seemingly impossible odds?

World War II Timeline

1933

Adolf Hitler is appointed chancellor of Germany; the first of dozens of concentration camps over Europe is established at the German village of Dachau.

1938

Germany invades Austria; Hitler holds his last annual rally in Nuremberg, which draws one million people who support his practices and ideals.

1939

Hitler invades Poland and Czechoslovakia, causing both countries to surrender; Nazis begin persecuting Polish Jews; the United States sells military supplies to British and France to support their efforts to oppose the Nazis; Great Britain, Australia, New Zealand, Canada, South Africa and India declare war on Germany in fall, making this the official start to World War II.

1940

Germany takes over Denmark, Norway, Belgium, Netherlands, Luxembourg, and France; Winston Churchill becomes Britain's new Prime Minister; Italy joins the war with Germany; the Battle of Britain begins when Germany bombs London and other British cities -- the 'Blitz' continues on London for 57 nights, killing more than 40,000 citizens; Japan joins Italy and Germany in fighting the Allies; American president Roosevelt is elected to a third term, the only time an American president will serve more than two terms; Roosevelt bans racial discrimination in war-industry employment.

1941

Germany invades Greece; the United States continues to send military equipment and other supplies to the Allies with payment deferred until after the war; Germany attacks the Soviet Union; the Soviet Union joins the Allies; Japan attacks Pearl Harbor, along with other Allied bases in the Pacific and Asia, the result being the United States and Great Britain declare war on Japan; Germany and Italy declare war on the United States.

1942

The Nazis establish a plan to kill European Jews via death camps; Japanese troops take control of large portions of East Asia and the Pacific, including Hong Kong, Singapore, the Philippines, Thailand, Malaysia and Burma; United States invades North Africa; United States wins the Battle of Midway, a major turning point in the war in the Pacific; people of Japanese heritage are interned in the United States.

1943

Italy is invaded by the Allies and surrenders; Mussolini is removed from power; Italy begins secret peace talks with the Allies and eventually declares war on Germany; Churchill, Roosevelt and Stalin meet to discuss Operation Overlord, the Allied invasion of Normandy, France, against Germany's armed forces.

1944

In January General Dwight D. Eisenhower takes charge of planning Operation Overlord, which takes place in June; Allies push German forces towards Germany, liberating many cities including Paris; Roosevelt is elected to his fourth term as United States president; in December, the Germans attempt a last-ditch effort to overcome the Allies by splitting their troops, a strategy that becomes known as the Battle of the Bulge; Allied island-hopping in the Pacific liberates the Philippines.

1945

Prisoners at Dachau and dozens of other death camps throughout Europe are freed; Allies defeat the Germans in the Battle of the Bulge; Allies take the Pacific island of Iwo Jima; Churchill, Roosevelt and Stalin meet for the last time in Yalta to discuss the end of the war and how to divide Germany; in April Roosevelt dies and Vice President Harry S. Truman is sworn in as president; Mussolini is captured and executed by his own people; Hitler commits suicide in his underground bunker in Berlin; Germany surrenders in May; Truman declares the end of the war on May 8 as V-E Day (Victory in Europe); United States drops atomic bombs on the Japanese cities of Hiroshima and Nagasaki; the Soviet Union declares war on Japan; Japan's Emperor Hirohito accepts the Allies' terms of surrender on August 14, which becomes known as V-J Day (Victory over Japan); American troops begin returning home, while others are assigned to Japan and Europe during the Allied period of occupation.

About the Author

Kayleen Reusser has written about hundreds of veterans. As a speaker, she presents talks about her World War II tour of Europe to groups. For more information go to

www.KayleenReusser.com.

Reusser's books are available on Amazon.

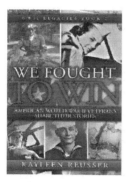 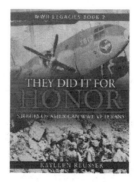 

Made in the USA
Lexington, KY
11 November 2019